The Brand-New Lawyer's Guide

The Brand-New Lawyer's Guide

to

Passing the Bar,
Learning the Trade,
and
Building a Sustainable Career

John W. Reilly
Brooklyn Law School

CAROLINA ACADEMIC PRESS
Durham, North Carolina

Library of Congress Cataloging-in-Publication Data

Names: Reilly, John W. author
Title: The brand-new lawyer's guide / John W. Reilly.
Description: Durham, North Carolina : Carolina Academic Press, 2025. | Includes bibliographical references and index.
Identifiers: LCCN 2025014860 | ISBN 9781531033415 paperback | ISBN 9781531033422 ebook
Subjects: LCSH: Law—Vocational guidance—United States | Practice of law—United States
Classification: LCC KF297 .R45 2025 | DDC 340.023/73—dc23 eng/20250401
LC record available at https://lccn.loc.gov/2025014860

Carolina Academic Press
700 Kent Street
Durham, North Carolina 27701
(919) 489-7486
www.cap-press.com

Printed in the United States of America

Contents

The Brand-New Lawyer's Guide

1
Introduction

It's 7:30 AM. I am standing on the 77th Street platform, waiting for the R train to take me into Manhattan. As part of my routine, I go through my checklist.

Job as a lawyer... check

Wear a nice suit to work... check

Work in a beautiful office in Manhattan... check

Three for three. Everything on the checklist has been completed. This is what I have strived for since I was a kid. As the R train pulls into the station, I continue my routine.

Is today the day I am going to throw myself in front of the R train so I don't have to step foot in that godforsaken office to endure another grueling 10-hour day?

The train pulls past me and comes to a complete stop.

No... check. I guess not.

I step onto the R train. The doors close. And, as the train moves, I count down the stops as if I'm counting down the number of seconds left before a bomb explodes or before my head is chopped off by a guillotine. The anxiety gets stronger the closer I get to Times Square. I wipe the sweat off my forehead and wish I could change my button-up shirt as I have already sweat through it.

I've waited my whole life to graduate from law school, pass the bar, and become a lawyer. Every step forward seemed to be better than the last. How did I reach the last step and fail so horribly? Why am I so miserable? Did I choose the wrong career path?

To say that my first few months after graduating law school were hectic (*and miserable*) would be an understatement.

Studied for the bar. Passed the bar. Started a job as a real estate lawyer. Quit after two months. Started a job as an Office of Foreign Assets Control (OFAC) Sanctions Compliance Officer. Started working remotely due to the COVID-19 pandemic. Contemplated taking a job as a family lawyer. And that was just the start.

As I navigated getting through each bump in the road, I continually searched online to see what resources there were for people who just graduated from law school, passed the bar exam, and didn't know what their next step should look like/were scared that they made the wrong career choice. I couldn't find a single resource.

So, I created my own.

This book is for people who are getting close to graduating from law school, people who just graduated from law school and are studying for the bar exam, or people who just passed the bar exam and are looking for their first legal job. This book contains my experiences, including some predicaments I found myself in the middle of, and some of the lessons I learned during my first five years as a lawyer. If you graduate from law school and find that you are unhappy career-wise, I hope that this book can help you to see that this unhappiness is not permanent. There are concrete steps you can take to move yourself and your career forward to a place where you feel satisfied and fulfilled.

This book is organized into sections corresponding to major events that occur after law school graduation. It starts by offering advice for bar prep. It then delves into finding your first job after law school and the key takeaways that should come out of that experience. It explores side hustles, volunteering, and networking. It discusses looking for your second legal job. Finally, it explores ways to perform an audit of your life and how to harmonize your career with the rest of your life.

2

Congratulations! You Graduated from Law School. Now Study for the Bar Exam.

NOTE: *In this chapter, "bar exam" refers to the Uniform Bar Exam (UBE).*

After years of studying, finals, internships, clinics, networking, and lots of hard work, graduating from law school feels like you have reached the light at the end of the tunnel. It is hard to explain how satisfying it is to finally be rewarded for all of the effort you put in, and only those who earn a JD diploma can truly know the feeling. Unfortunately, another feeling that only law school graduates can truly understand is the anxiety of sitting for the bar exam.

The bar exam is the final hurdle that law school graduates must overcome before they can officially hold themselves out as lawyers and practice in the legal arena. Unfortunately for some, it is a pesky hurdle that needs to be repeated more than once to pass.

For law school graduates who want to practice law after graduation, passing the bar is a must. (On the contrary, those who are looking for opportunities outside of being a lawyer have no need to take the bar exam. Woohoo! You can move on to the next chapter.) There are steps that law school graduates can take to maximize their chances of passing the bar exam. Some of these steps include

(1) taking a pre-bar class as a 3L; (2) studying with a commercial bar prep course; (3) taking additional timed-practice tests; (4) taking breaks that maximize stress relief; and (5) creating a schedule and sticking to it.

Take a Pre-Bar Class

One way that people can get a head start on studying for the bar exam is by taking a pre-bar class offered by their law school. These courses can vary from law school to law school, but the gist is the same: students are taught materials that will be on the bar exam. In addition to serving as a refresher for the black-letter law studied during the first-year and in other elective courses, these pre-bar classes provide invaluable guidance on how to draft essay answers and how to analyze multiple-choice questions.

So much of what is taught in law school does not neatly translate to the bar exam. As students work through upper-level courses, they find themselves either taking finals or writing papers for classes during the final few weeks of the semester. They are focused on one area of law per exam or paper, so they don't have to switch gears (by subject or type of question). For finals, they study for their class, sit down to take a three-hour exam, and then move on to study for the next class. For papers, students can spend as much (or as little) time as they want to find relevant material and write. They have the option to, and are encouraged to, proofread and update their papers as much as they want—they do not (necessarily) have to deal with a time-crunch.

The finals period usually lasts about three weeks; the suggested study time for the bar exam is about ten weeks.

In short, the bar exam is a totally different beast.

The UBE tests 12 subjects (a mix of doctrinal and elective courses) and is broken into three different sections: (1) the multistate performance test (MPT) (closed-universe essay questions, such as memos, briefs, or persuasive letters); (2) the multistate essay exam (MEE) (issue-spotting and memory-recall essay questions); and (3) the multistate bar exam (MBE) (multiple-choice questions). This exam requires test takers to memorize endless black-letter laws, change gears from subject to subject, and employ different strategies for addressing each of the three question types. In my experience, there are not many law school classes that address building and practicing all of these skills at once.

The class that comes closest to addressing all of these skills in preparation for the bar exam is a pre-bar class. (Shocking, right?!) Third-year law students can take a pre-bar class for one or two semesters in order to get a head start on bar exam preparation. These classes can help them to (1) become familiar with the exam format and exam strategies and (2) develop study resources for memorizing black-letter law that can be used during commercial bar prep.

Before sitting down for my first pre-bar class during my last semester of law school, I had no idea what was on the bar exam. All I knew is that it was a big, metaphorical band aid that I wanted to rip off quickly and be done with as soon as possible. To my dismay, I was (correctly) informed during that first class that studying for the bar exam is a marathon, not a sprint. *So, I wouldn't be ripping off of that big, metaphorical band aid as quickly as I was hoping.*

That first pre-bar class did more than enlighten me regarding the pace of studying for the bar exam. It provided me with details about what would be needed to successfully prepare myself for the bar exam.

Bar Exam. Two Days.

MPT (20% total grade) Day 1—Morning

MEE (30% total grade) Day 1—Afternoon

MBE (50% (!!!) total grade) Day 3—Morning and Afternoon

I scribbled my notes down as quickly as I could type them into the tiny Bluetooth keyboard that connected to my iPad.

Two days? And one of them is completely filled with multiple-choice? What did I get myself into?

Before that first class, I had no idea what would be on the bar exam. *How did I not research all of this earlier!?* After that first class, I left with a clear picture of the enormous task ahead of me. And more importantly, I left with clear expectations of what was going to be on the exam and a clear idea of how I could start preparing for it now, six months before the actual exam date.

In addition to realizing how important it was to familiarize myself with the exam format, I learned the importance of having a strategy for each type of question.

One story about reviewing MPTs still sticks out to me to this day.

MPTs provide test takers with a task memo, a file, and a library. The task memo includes the essay prompt and overall question(s) that the student needs to answer. *Do I need to write an objective legal brief? Do I need to write a persuasive letter to a judge?* The file provides test takers with the facts of the case. *Sometimes this comes in the form of a deposition or notes from another lawyer who did client intake for this case.* The library provides the law that is relevant to the case. *It can be in the form black-letter law definitions or case law from actual cases.*

The instructor posed the following question: "So, in front of us we have an MPT. We are presented with a task memo, a file, and a library. Which order should we read them in?"

Well, probably the task memo, file, and library, if that's the order we received it. Did I pass the bar yet?

"If you said task memo, file, library, you may be right. But if you said task memo, library, file, you may be right, too. Some people process information better by learning the facts and then the law (file then library) and some people process information better by reviewing the law and then the facts (library then file). Try both strategies as we move forward and see which one works best for you."

I was stunned when I heard that information. If the bar examiners are giving us this information in a specific order, it must be for a reason. Why would I try to mess that up? At the suggestion of my pre-bar professor, I did try both ways. To my surprise, I processed information better by reading about the law before reading the file. (I would still swear by this method, but as my professor who is much smarter than me noted, it depends on the individual taking the exam.)

Allowing myself time to take multiple practice tests and develop my strategy was of paramount importance to my success during post-graduation bar prep and on the bar exam. Time is either your best friend or your worst enemy when it comes to studying for the bar exam. Nothing can be crammed overnight. The hard work people put in day in and day out translates into passing the bar exam.

And speaking of time, the second great thing you get from enrolling in a pre-bar course is the time to study and develop resources for learning the black-letter law that will be tested on the bar exam.

Continuing with the marathon analogy, it takes time and practice to develop the memorization skills required to prepare for the bar exam. In my experience, apart from some 1L year courses, not many law school classes require students to take a closed-book exam. People who study for the bar exam not only have to practice a skill they haven't used in at least two years but also have to memorize seemingly endless black-letter law.

To say this task is daunting is the understatement of all understatements.

Memorizing the black-letter law for one topic is challenging enough, let alone multiplying that by 12 subjects. And so a law school pre-bar class will teach you how to break down a subject and topic into bite-sized pieces—a skill that is transferable to post-graduation bar exam prep. Pre-bar classes, which span only one or two semesters, cannot fit an entire bar exam's worth of information into a syllabus. (And they certainly should not try to!) But what they can do, by covering a few select subjects, questions, and strategies, is help people to identify their strengths and weaknesses, allow for practice and repetition, and help people to build confidence in their exam-taking skills.

For example, most pre-bar courses will tackle three to four doctrinal subjects in a semester, reviewing a combination of MPT, MEE, and MBE questions for each subject. For MEE and MBE questions, having the black-letter law memorized is extremely helpful with legal analysis and drawing the proper conclusion. For MEE questions in particular, being able to identify the rule statement, i.e., the R in IRAC (Issue-Rule-Application-Conclusion) analysis, is a necessary step in formulating a successful answer.

In a pre-bar class, students memorize manageable sets of black-letter law. This can help to relieve some of the pressure that is associated with having to memorize 12 areas of law. It also allows students to put together resources that will continue to help them even after the semester ends. Outlines, flash cards, and practice questions are all vital elements of successful bar exam preparation.

My pre-bar course covered contracts, real property, and evidence, and it included both multiple-choice questions and essay questions. (Side note: pre-bar courses at other law schools may teach this class differently. Some will cover all topics in the MBE section during the semester. Others will cover only MEEs or MPTs during the semester. Case in point: these classes can be taught a variety of ways.) When studying for the final exam for my course, I created color-coded flash cards to help me memorize the relevant laws. This study habit carried over to my studying post-graduation and helped to keep me organized and confident as I prepared for the bar exam. Having multicolored stacks of black-letter law allowed me to break up the course into more bite-sized pieces and to hone in on areas that needed more of my attention. Additionally, when I would begin to review a topic that I had previously covered in my pre-bar course, I'd get a much needed confidence boost upon realizing that I already had a comfortable mastery over the topic.

There are many aspects of law school that are mandatory—attending doctrinal courses during your 1L year, interning in different legal capacities, completing writing requirements—but attending a pre-bar course is not necessarily one of them. However, I strongly recommend taking a pre-bar course before graduating from law school. These courses help to demystify the bar exam and allow law students to begin to strategize, memorize, and develop the confidence needed to pass the bar exam on the first attempt.

Choosing a Commercial Bar Prep Course

"So, who do you think you're going to be studying with over the summer? BARBRI, Themis, Kaplan, Pieper?"

I've never heard a kindergarten teacher in the hipster Brooklyn neighborhood of Park Slope go through roll call, but I imagine this is what it sounds like.

"Hmm...I'm still not sure yet. I'm looking into it."

"Better pick one out soon! Summer is just around the corner!"

Do I really even need to do this....

Commercial bar prep courses are often the subject of lively debate within law schools. Which program is best? When should you sign up for a program? Which one have most students already signed up for? How did students from last year's graduating class do? Who's handing out free MPRE (Multistate Professional Responsibility Exam) books in the cafeteria? The list goes on and on.

The good news about selecting a bar prep company is that they all generally provide the same information. The bad news about selecting a bar prep company is that they all generally provide the same information. What makes a difference is the time and effort people are able to spend on these courses.

First, you may be thinking: When should I start looking into bar prep courses? As early as my 1L year? As a 3L right before graduation? You'll hear lots of chatter about when to sign up for a bar prep course. Some suggest signing up for a commercial bar prep course as a 1L because bar prep companies often will give students a slight discount for signing up early. However, my advice is to select a course during the beginning of your last semester of your 3L year. Waiting until your 3L year provides more time to see the different options that are available and to select the course that is the best fit for you as the bar exam becomes a top priority. *Also, life can be so unpredictable between your 1L year and 3L year. Holding off on a decision until you know when you will be graduating and when you will be taking the bar exam may save you a headache down the line.*

A common, and overused, metaphor for the bar exam (one I've mentioned twice already) is "The bar is a marathon, not a sprint." *Heads up: I will continue to overuse this metaphor throughout this book.* Over the course of 9 to 10 weeks, law school graduates are tasked with learning, memorizing, and explaining 12 different areas of law. That is no small feat. The major companies that provide bar preparation have seen thousands of people study for the bar exam using their materials, and these companies are constantly tweaking those learning aids to help law school graduates learn, memorize, and explain these laws. *As a result of their having so much data, these companies basically have bar exam prep down to a science.*

There are other, more minor, aspects that you might take into account when trying to decide among the different bar prep providers. One of these is how many of your peers are using certain bar prep programs. Being part of a bar prep program that many other people you know have also chosen can be beneficial if you like group study sessions and will use these group sessions to hold yourself accountable. However, if you prefer to study alone or tend to get easily distracted by studying with other people, you may be better off selecting a bar prep course that is less popular among your peers, making it easier for you to work independently and maintain focus.

As you consider bar prep providers, you may also want to take into account whether your school provides any special accommodations to certain ones, for example, whether it permits certain bar prep providers to screen their lectures inside law school classrooms. This type of arrangement could be attractive if you prefer to study on campus and maintain a schedule where you can get up early, go to school, and begin studying for the day. However, if you prefer to study off campus, whether from home or at a coffee shop, this type of arrangement may not be a selling point. Whether such an agreement between a bar prep provider and a law school is a pro or a con will come down to personal preference.

Another aspect you may wish to take into account is the format of the preparation, i.e., how the information is provided and presented. Nowadays, for the most part, and especially post-pandemic, most bar prep companies make information accessible from an online portal. While most of these portals have similar interfaces, they are not identical, and so some people may find certain interfaces to be more user-friendly than others. Exploring the different websites and portals before making a decision is therefore worthwhile, and I advise doing so before selecting a bar prep provider. Most of these companies offer free guides and help with the MPRE and also for studying for different 1L courses; familiarizing oneself with the different bar prep companies at these stages may help making the decision for bar prep easier.

Back when I was studying for the bar exam, I chose a course that broadcast its lectures at my law school. That format appealed to me because I am the type of person who is most productive when I must stick to a schedule and leave my apartment. Also, because the lectures took place at school, many of my peers also chose the same program. I found that discussing daily legal topics and exchanging notes with fellow students was very helpful. However, if I were the type of person who finds studying with and talking to other people to be anxiety inducing, this may not have been a great option for me.

Selecting a bar prep company feels like a very important decision. *And it is.* But take comfort in knowing that most of the material will be the same no matter which provider you choose. The most important thing is that you devote yourself to studying and practicing the materials so that you can pass the bar exam on the first try.

What Does Bar Prep Look Like?

Those who do not take a pre-bar course during their last year of law school will be introduced to bar prep materials through their post-graduation commercial bar course. During the course, they will, for the first time, learn about the structure of the exam and how much effort and strategy must go into studying for it. Often, people who take this path become overwhelmed by the amount of information covered on the exam, how much they need to learn, and what they need to do to pass the bar exam. Having at least some knowledge of the exam's content and structure before sitting down for your first commercial bar prep course could help to alleviate some of this stress.

All bar prep companies structure their courses similarly. Each legal subject that needs to be taught is broken down into lectures across two to three days, and a detailed agenda for each day is provided. The day begins with a three-hour morning lecture, give or take (sometimes a lecture may be closer to four hours, and other times it may be under three). After each lecture, students spend time answering multiple-choice questions and completing different essay exercises in order to test their understanding of the law and to see whether they can explain it in writing. It takes about six weeks for a course to cover all areas of the law that are tested on the bar. The final three to four weeks involve lots of practice questions, including essays, multiple-choice questions, and MPT questions. These exercises are integrated into study plans so that students can practice applying their knowledge to different types of questions and then have time to review their mistakes in depth. The course also includes a full-day "midterm" that comprises 200 multiple-choice questions. Students grade their own work and then try to identify their strengths and weaknesses in terms of the MBE subjects.

One of the most daunting aspects of bar prep is the memorization phase, which typically kicks into high gear after week six. (Not that students aren't beginning to memorize during the first part of the course—it's just that students are no longer learning or relearning areas of law in the second part of the course and are instead fully focused on memorizing what they (re)learned.) Memorization is great preparation for multiple-choice questions and can help in identifying what legal issues are being presented. It is also helpful for the MEE portion of the bar exam, where test takers must recall the black-letter law and use it to analyze the legal issues at hand.

You may at times believe that you do not have enough information or legal knowledge to attempt to answer different essay questions or multiple-choice questions. But you are mistaken. It is not unusual to feel this way; however, learning occurs through the trial and error of answering these different practice questions. The sooner you tackle these practice questions, the sooner you can identify your areas of strength and areas that require more focus and improvement. Bar prep companies have developed more practice questions than most people can even complete during a 10-week course, which means it's nearly impossible to run out of information or practice materials to help you strengthen any areas of weakness.

Getting Ready to Sit for the Bar Exam

Another true but overused saying is "The time you put into studying for this exam is what you get out of it." Because it is terribly difficult to study, learn, and memorize the many different subjects and laws that may appear on the bar exam, you are likely to feel anxiety as the date of the bar exam draws closer. But you may also feel some relief that soon the exam will be behind you. Regardless, the best thing that you can do for yourself is put in the time to study, day in and day out, from day one. It is not possible to memorize and adequately prepare for this exam over the course of a few days or a week, so it is up to you to make every day of this 10-week process count. Those who adhere to their agendas and plans, and who put in the time to study, are more likely to feel confident as they sit down for the bar exam.

It is impossible to predict what legal topics the bar exam will present. Maybe you will recall a lot about a certain topic that is presented and feel comfortable answering the question. But maybe you won't be as familiar with other topics and will have to use whatever knowledge you do have to craft an answer. Regardless, sitting for a two-day bar exam is a herculean task, and you should feel proud of yourself for completing it.

When I was preparing for the bar exam, I found that making certain actions part of my daily routine helped me to stick to my study schedule. I found that taking a mid-day walk to go and get coffee enabled me to make the most of my study time in the library. This ten-minute walk—and the caffeine—broke up my day a bit and allowed me to re-energize and re-focus. Having a regular workout routine also helped. I'll be the first to admit that, even though I tried my best, I did not always stick to a workout routine during law school—but when it came to those ten weeks leading up to the bar exam, I stuck to it. Because it's easier to do something you actually enjoy, my workout of choice was spinning classes. Two or three times a week, I would head to spinning class after a long day of studying. These classes symbolized the end of a successful day of studying. In them, I was able to focus entirely on spinning, release my pent-up energy, and take a mental break before having to begin the studying process again the next day.

These strategies will look different for everyone. Some people unwind at the end of the day by watching their favorite show. Some people love to call and catch up with their family and friends to see how their days are going. Some people like going to the gym or taking walks. Whatever your preferred stress outlet may be, putting together a schedule that includes planned breaks and sets aside time for stress-releasing activities can be incredibly helpful in helping you to keep your sanity as you prepare for the bar. Additionally, incorporating planned breaks into your study routine and viewing them as part of your daily objectives can allow you to avoid any guilt you might otherwise feel for not dedicating 100 percent of your time to studying.

Taking the Bar Exam

When the day finally came for me to sit for the bar exam, my hands trembled as I opened the first MPT question. I had studied diligently and I was prepared. Yet, as I sat there, I couldn't help but tremble. *I spent the past ten weeks preparing for this moment, and now that it's here, I go into a state of shock. How convenient!* But as I took some deep breaths and began to read through the question, my nervousness started to dissipate. As I began to identify the different issues that were being presented and develop the outline for my written response, my fears subsided, replaced by confidence.

When I finished the exam and walked out of the massive Jacob Javits Convention Center (*3.3 million square feet to be precise*) at the end of the second day, I could hardly believe that I was done. I felt both exhaustion and excitement as a result of finally finishing this gargantuan task.

And then the waiting game began. *Nooooooo. I already took the exam! Why do they make us wait so long?!* Waiting to see my score and find out whether I had passed was almost as difficult as studying for the bar exam itself. *Did I pass? Did I fail?* Depending on where you take the July exam, you may find out as early as September, or as late as October or November. If you take the February exam, you usually will find out around April or May. Learning that you passed the bar exam brings on a huge sense of relief, success, and pride. You will never have to take an exam like this again. And you are one step closer to practicing as a lawyer. *Woohoo! All the hard work did pay off!* And so begins the next phase—finding a job.

3

I Passed the Bar Exam! Why Am I Not Officially a Lawyer Yet?

Once you've finished celebrating passing the bar exam, your next step will be to apply to the bar of the particular state (*or federal district... Hi, Washington, DC!... or territories... Hi, Guam and Puerto Rico!*) you wish to practice in. "Almost-lawyers" must apply to the bar of the jurisdiction in which they plan to work so that they can practice law officially (read: *legally*). Once almost-lawyers are admitted to the bar, they become lawyers (*yay!*).

The bar admission process varies by state. Some states require piles of documentation and multiple exams, while others require only a passing bar exam score and submission of a character and fitness application. After passing the bar exam, the first jurisdiction I applied to was New York, one of the states having many requirements for bar admission. (*Sigh.... I thought passing the bar was supposed to be the hard part.... Why is New York State torturing me with more exams and a long application process?... sigh again.*)

The next few pages recount my personal experience with the bar admission process in New York State (and beyond).

Uniform Bar Exam

Let's start with the obvious. You need to pass the Uniform Bar Exam to become a lawyer in New York. (**Record scratch* What?!... I know that this probably comes as a surprise to you, especially after the previous chapter.*) However, this exam is not the only one you need to pass in order to become a lawyer in New York.

Multistate Professional Responsibility Examination

The Multistate Professional Responsibility Examination (MPRE) is a professional and ethical exam for lawyers. Per the MPRE website, the MPRE "is a two-hour, 60-question multiple-choice examination [including 10 experimental questions] that is administered three times per year. Developed by the National Conference of Bar Examiners (NCBE), the MPRE is required for admission to the bars of all but two US jurisdictions (Wisconsin and Puerto Rico). (Note that Connecticut and New Jersey accept successful completion of a law school course on professional responsibility in lieu of a passing score on the MPRE.)"[1]

MPRE scores are reported on a scale of 50 (low) to 150 (high).[2] Passing scores are established by each jurisdiction, ranging from 75 to 86. The passing score in most jurisdictions is 85. Furthermore, each jurisdiction sets its own MPRE maximum age policy. In New York, MPRE exam scores are valid for four years from the date of the exam.

I first learned of the MPRE during law school. Multiple times throughout the year, various bar prep companies would set up tables with stacks of free MPRE practice books for students (*for those who signed up to receive emails and updates from said bar company... there is always a price*). I signed up for all of the different email lists so that I could have multiple books to practice with—the more study materials you have, the better. But these books were more than just MPRE study resources. They served as helpful introduc-

1. https://www.ncbex.org/exams/mpre
2. https://www.ncbex.org/exams/mpre/mpre-scores

tions to the various bar prep websites and companies, making it easier to select a bar prep provider down the line. For these reasons, I recommend this approach—collecting as many MPRE practice books from as many bar prep providers as possible—to anyone who will need to take the MPRE.

Each MPRE practice book contains study guides and practice questions for each of the different topics the exam covers (e.g., conflicts of interest, lawyer-client relationship, legal malpractice). Each book also contains one to three practice exams that students can take under timed conditions. As with the bar exam, the more time you spend studying and preparing for the MPRE, the better you will do on the exam.

One piece of advice someone gave me was to study for and sign up for the MPRE in the same semester as my required legal ethics class. In my experience, this was good advice. The legal ethics class covered most of the topics that would be covered on the MPRE, and studying for the MPRE helped me to prepare for my legal ethics final. Doing things this way basically doubled the benefits of my studying efforts.

Some people decide to take the MPRE during law school, while others choose to take it after the bar exam, for a host of reasons (such as they didn't have time during the school year, or didn't pass it the first time around). [Note: Some jurisdictions require that you pass the MPRE before sitting for the bar exam.] I would recommend against waiting until after the bar exam to take the MPRE. In fact, I strongly recommend knocking out the MPRE before sitting for the bar exam. Why? Because the bar exam is such a slog that you'll probably never want to take another exam again. It will therefore be difficult to get back into the right headspace to study for yet another exam after you've taken the bar (*not impossible, of course, but difficult*).

The New York Law Course and New York Law Exam

As if studying for and passing the bar exam and the MPRE were not enough to drive law students crazy, New York State also requires law students to take and pass the New York Law Exam (NYLE). The

NYLE is a 50-question, multiple-choice test that takes two hours. It covers most of the same topics as the uniform bar exam but also includes professional responsibility and administrative law. *As the name of the exam suggests, all of these legal topics are covered from a New York point of view.* The test is offered four times per year, and a minimum score of 60 percent is required to pass.

In order to be eligible to sit for this exam, you must first register and take the New York Law Course (NYLC). The NYLC is a series of videos and quizzes on each area of law covered on the NYLE. Per the New York Bar exam website:

> When viewing the lectures the first time, applicants will be required to answer questions during the course of each lecture, to assure that they are attentive to and gaining an understanding of the material presented. Once the embedded question to any given segment is answered correctly, that segment cannot be re-watched until the entire course is completed.[3]

As a law student from New York, I found the course itself to be quite interesting. A lot of the courses I took in law school offered a global or federal perspective on the law, so getting to learn about the intricacies of the New York legal system was fun for me.

That being said, the NYLC was tough at times. For one thing, it was time consuming. It has approximately 17 hours' worth of videos, broken down by legal topic, that need to be completed. Quiz questions embedded in each video must be answered correctly in order to continue the lecture. Any time I gave an incorrect answer and had to rewatch a video, a little piece of me died. (*Dramatic? Yes. But that's how it feels in the moment!*) One aspect of the NYLC that I did like was how it did not force you to watch groups of videos within a set (and short) period of time. Instead, to be eligible to register for the exam, you simply had to complete all videos by the registration deadline, which is generally around a month before the exam date.

---

3. https://www.nybarexam.org/Content/CourseMaterials.htm

I treated studying for this exam like most other open-book exams. I watched the videos, took notes, and did practice quizzes. Most people I knew who had already taken the exam advised me that it was not overly difficult, and so I tried not to stress out too much about it.

The NYLE is administered remotely, which means that test-takers have to download the NYLE software onto their computers. I decided to take the exam at home, from the comfort of my own desk. I had the official NYLC notes as well as my own on hand, in case I needed to reference them. As I began to answer the questions, I thought that they seemed harder than I had expected. After I had finished, I was not sure how to feel. *Neither passing nor failing will be a surprise to me... that's probably bad, right?*

Luckily, I didn't have too wait to long for my test results because the New York Bar (usually) gets scores back to people within two weeks. Luckily, I passed on my first try. Interestingly, if you pass on the first attempt, you do not get a score report—you are simply told that you passed. So I could have received the minimum passing score 60 percent (*likely*), or I could have received a perfect score of 100 percent (*not likely*). I'll never know.

Those who do not pass the NYLE on the first attempt will need to retake both the NYLC and NYLE.

Character and Fitness Application and Interview

A woman from the Bar Association Department of the court came to my law school to tell all the 3Ls about applying for the bar exam. She looked just like Roz from Disney's *Monster's Inc.* (Disclaimer: She may not have looked like this. But this is how I remember her.) She was older and grumpy.

Every statement she made sounded like a curt warning: *Don't lie on the application! Don't have any ambiguities on the application! If there are any discrepancies, we'll send it back to you, and you'll need to re-submit it!*

Oh my God, lady. Take a chill pill!

As I scribbled down my notes, I remember being shocked when she said that about 90 percent of applications are sent back to the applicant for corrections and must be resubmitted. *That's a preposterous number! There is no way I am going to be part of that group.*

After passing the bar exam and completing the other requirements, I began to complete all the required paperwork for the New York Bar application. The application itself must be filled out by the applicant, and it asks for all the usual stuff: personal information, education history, work and internship history, criminal history, and military history. But it also asks for some more unusual information, such as whether you are involved in any civil litigation and whether you have had any dealings with law enforcement. It also famously (*infamously?*) asks whether you, the applicant, have ever tried to overthrow the United States government.

The applicant must also provide two good moral character affirmations. An affirmant should be someone who has known the applicant for at least two years and can attest to the applicant's character. Each of these individuals must fill out a character and fitness form stating their belief that the applicant has the character and fitness to be a successful lawyer. Additionally, for any law-related employment, the applicant's supervisor must fill out a form attesting that the applicant performed good work.

Getting these forms filled out by colleagues and former supervisors is a lesson in organization and can be a real pain. It is tough to keep track of multiple documents and make sure that they are filled out properly before appending them to the main application. But this process also provides a great opportunity to reconnect with former supervisors and share the good news that you passed the bar exam. I was fortunate that my former supervisors were all responsive to my asks and filled out the forms in a timely manner. If your former supervisors are not being responsive, it is okay to be persistent and follow-up on your original emails—you need to become a lawyer! (This process is also a great way to network, stay in touch, and keep former supervisors up-to-date of your accomplishments even after you have been admitted to the bar.)

In addition to the application and recommendations, New York State also has a 50-hour pro bono requirement (*pretty self-explanatory—you must have a supervisor (or supervisors) sign off on the fact that you completed 50 hours or more of pro bono services*), a skills form affidavit (*perhaps not as self-explanatory—the law school submits this form to confirm that the applicant has the basic competence and ethical participation to be a lawyer*), and a law school certificate (*pretty self-explanatory—your law school confirms with the bar that you graduated from law school).*

Once I submitted my completed application, I anxiously checked my inbox every day (*strike that—more like every half hour)* for an email asking me to schedule my character and fitness interview. After weeks of waiting, I finally received an email, but to my surprise, it was not about scheduling an interview. Instead, it informed me that my application had some errors and needed to be resubmitted. (*Damn it! Roz tried to warn me but I didn't listen!!!*) One error was that my signature was not the same on all documents (some documents I had signed John Reilly, while others I had signed John W. Reilly). I was told to pick one and stick with it. The other error involved one of the forms filled out by a previous supervisor: she referred to me as an associate even though I had been just an intern. I had to go back to that supervisor and have her sign off on an updated version of the recommendation that contained the proper reference. I was able to correct the errors pretty quickly and resubmit my application. Shortly thereafter, I received the email I had been waiting for—I finally had a character and fitness interview on the schedule.

Once the interview was officially on the calendar, I began to prepare for different types of questions that I might be asked. I started by searching Google for sample questions. Some questions were what you'd expect ("Explain why you think you'll be a good lawyer," and "Tell me about your law school experience"), but others caused some anxiety ("Why is there a gap on your resume?" and "Explain this blemish on your record"). I did my best to block out the horror stories about interviews gone wrong.

I reviewed my copy of my application and (*thankfully*) did not have any major blemishes on my application to write about. *I hav-*

en't been fired, I've never been arrested, and I've never tried to overthrow the U.S. Government. But what if they find something that I'm not seeing?! Although I was nervous there might be a "gotcha" question, I continued to focus my energies on preparing for possible interview questions.

On the day of my interview, I looked at myself in the mirror, dressed in a full suit and tie, and took a deep breath. *It's time.* I then began the long commute from my bedroom to my kitchen table, where I logged on to Zoom. (Did I mention that all of this was happening during the COVID-19 lockdown? My interview was virtual.) The interview began shortly after I signed on, and it was, thankfully, short and sweet. The interviewer complimented my resume and application, told me that she saw no red flags, and asked whether I had any questions for her. I asked her some general questions about practicing law in New York and about transitioning from law school to working full time, and she indulged me with some stories about her law practice and career. She ended the interview by letting me know that there would be a few follow-up emails about the swearing-in ceremony. *Woohoo! I'm almost there! I'm almost a lawyer!*

Swearing-In Ceremony

A little over a week after my character and fitness interview, I was being sworn into the New York Bar! I and other future lawyers who had completed all the bar admission requirements would be sworn in over Zoom (*clearly not the typical swearing-in ceremony.*) Normally, friends and family attend the swearing-in ceremony to watch their loved one take the Attorney's Oath, sign their name into the book of lawyers, and officially become a lawyer.

Earlier, I had once again put on a full suit and tie and sat down at my kitchen table. The court held a brief ceremony in which it emphasized the importance of the legal profession and how we would persevere through the turbulent pandemic and improve the legal profession. The ceremony concluded with a reminder from the clerk of the court to sign a PDF version of the Attorney's Oath and send it back to her—we would not be official lawyers until we had done so. (*Just when you think there are no more hurdles to clear, a new one gets added.*) Afterward, I quickly printed out the Attorney's Oath, signed it, and sent it back to the clerk.

I changed out of my suit into some comfy gym clothes, sat on my couch, and took a bite out of a peanut butter and jelly sandwich. *Alright! I'm a lawyer! Is this what being a layer is supposed to feel like?—I wasn't really sure.*

Reciprocity

Examinees who passed the Uniform Bar Exam and are already admitted to practice in one jurisdiction have three years from their test date to use their test score to transfer into other jurisdictions that also accept the Uniform Bar Exam. Not everyone feels the need to transfer into any other jurisdictions *(plus, getting admitted into one jurisdiction is already a herculean effort...no need to do that again!)*, but some benefit from taking advantage of this reciprocity. For example, folks who practice real estate law in New York also choose to get admitted to the New Jersey bar because many clients own property in both states.

After getting admitted to the New York bar, I knew I also wanted to get admitted to the New Jersey bar and the Washington, D.C., bar. Waiving into New Jersey made sense geographically, but the Washington, D.C., bar was appealing to me for two reasons: One, I had gone down to D.C. a bunch of times to visit family who live in the area, and I really loved it. Two, life is unpredictable, and if I ever needed to live somewhere other than New York, Washington, D.C., is somewhere I could see myself living and working. *And Florida, if you accepted the complete Uniform Bar Exam and did not have any other state requirements, I would have waived into your jurisdiction, too!*

Because New York has so many requirements for gaining admittance to the bar, I had already done most of the work that was needed to waive into these jurisdictions. That was a pro. But repeating this process over and over again would be time consuming and costly. That was a con. Though I celebrated becoming a lawyer in New York, I still didn't feel like I had made it to the mountain top.

My desk was littered with to-do lists, status updates, and budgets to make sure that I was moving these processes along. But I stayed on top of these to-do lists and slowly but surely submitted each element of the application until all I had left to do was play the waiting game. Thankfully, both applications were admitted on the first submission. (*Shout out to the New York Bar admissions team for teaching me what it really means to cross every "t" and dot every "i" before submitting an application to a legal body.*)

For all three bar admissions, I received a formal law license on diploma-like paper showing that I was admitted to practice law in the jurisdiction. Whenever one would arrive in the mail, I'd try putting it into various frames lying around my house until I found the closest fit. Though none of the frames were the perfect size, looking at my licenses brought me a sense of pride and accomplishment that I had not experienced before. For years, I spent all my time and effort on getting into law school, graduating, passing the bar exam, and becoming a lawyer. And now I was. I finally did it. I jumped through every hoop, cleared every hurdle, passed every test, and signed my name to the Attorney's Oath. I have the law licenses to prove it.

I took my law licenses and brought them into my bedroom, where my college and law school diplomas hung over a desk cluttered with papers, to-do lists, and sticky notes covering every inch of available space. I then hung up my imperfectly framed law licenses alongside my diplomas (*but first I prayed that I would not put any unnecessary holes in the wall*). I stopped to take a look at the wall and take it all in. *I finally did it. Not only did I become a lawyer, but I became a lawyer in three different jurisdictions. No more tests, no more admissions fees, no more waiting for application updates.* Even though I knew I had a long journey ahead, I knew that I was prepared and ready to tackle any of the challenges that the legal profession threw my way.[4]

---

4. Note to reader: I was neither prepared nor ready for all the challenges that the legal profession was going to throw my way.

4

Networking and Finding a Job after Law School

The experience of finding a job after law school varies from person to person. *And it varies big time.* Those who work in big law firms during their 2L summer are often able to quickly secure a job offer by the end of that summer. But those who do not take the big law route need much more time to secure a job offer: some may accept a position before bar prep begins, and some may not find a position until they are studying for the bar exam. The most likely scenario, however, is that most will not secure a position until after passing the bar exam, as most employers are only interested in candidates who have already done so. For folks who fall into this last category, finding a position can feel like an insanely drawn-out process.

This chapter focuses on looking for a job after students have already passed the bar exam.

Where to Look

Since the point of going to law school is to secure a job in the legal field, you may wonder why more future lawyers don't start job searching while they are studying for the bar exam. Well, if there's any lesson you should have learned in Chapter 3, it's that the bar exam and bar prep is all-encompassing. Maybe it strikes you as counterintuitive not to job search during bar prep, but the reality is that securing a job offer during this time can be difficult—in part because of the overwhelming commitment that bar prep entails and in part because the odds of finding an employer who will hire someone who hasn't yet passed the bar exam are relatively low. But just because you should wait doesn't mean that you shouldn't keep an open eye, look at job portals, and do online searches.

A great place to start a job search is on job search portals through your law school. You can start doing these searches well before you graduate or begin to study for the bar exam. Browsing these portals is a way to see what types of jobs are out there, which can help you to narrow or define your career plans.

Who to Look For

Perhaps even more important than searching on job portals is building a network. Now, I know that some people hear the word "networking" and cringe. *And I get it.* Networking is not fun for everyone. And, during the pandemic, networking had to be done online, which made it feel very impersonal. But even now, when things have mostly gone back to normal, networking can still feel disheartening. As a law student or someone who just recently passed the bar exam, you may feel as if you don't have much to offer in terms of a networking relationship—and that's normal. However, don't let this stop you from developing your network and experience.

Networking does not have to be as intimidating as some make it out to be. Breaking it down into bite-sized pieces before rushing headfirst into a stereotypical roomful of lawyers holding drinks and making small talk could help make it more manageable. You might not realize it at first, but members of your school are part of your network. This includes not only your peers but also professors, academic success professionals, and career counselors. Start building your network by reaching out to a professor whose class you really enjoyed. Or reach out an academic success professional who helps with essay writing. Or reach out to your career counselor. Or just ask a classmate to reconnect over a cup of coffee.

As beginner's exercise, identify one person whose career you are interested in learning more about and reach out to them to set up an informal chat. Using my life as an example, I had worked with a career counselor during my 1L and 2L summer searches for legal internships. She was familiar with my resume and the types of law that I was interested in pursuing. Making an appointment with her to discuss career options was immeasurably helpful in my job search.

Speaking with a career counselor and close advisers as you are trying to decide what type of law to pursue after law school is so important. Many students enter law school with a general interest in the law but no concrete ideas about what type of law they want to practice. As they continue to take classes, the type of law they want to pursue often becomes apparent. This, however, was not my experience. Prior to entering law school, I had some internship experience in real estate law and thought that I would pursue this area of law after graduation. But, as I took more classes, participated in clinics, and gained more internship experience, I discovered that I also loved international law, LGBTQ+ law, and family law. In fact, after my 1L real property class, I never took another property law class again. The closer I got to graduating from law school, the more torn I felt about my future law career. *Oh my God, what am I going to do with my life?!* Though I was very interested in international, LGBTQ+, and family law, I had concerns about each: Could I even find a job in international law? Could I financially support myself if I pursued LGBTQ+ law or family law? Was I even all that interested in real estate law? I had to sort through a lot of pros and cons.

My biggest mistake was suppressing my conflicting feelings instead of addressing them head-on. Instead of discussing my concerns with my career counselor, I took what I thought was a practical approach: "I think I'm interested in international law, but I don't think I can find a job in that area. So for now I want to look for something in real estate law." Instead of helping me to work through my inner conflicts, my career counselor focused on helping me to find positions in real estate law that would accept someone right out of law school. And she did a wonderful job—I was quickly put in touch with a clinical law professor who worked in real estate and had a list of alumni who were willing to talk to different students. I was able to search for them on the web, reach out to them via email, and ultimately set up calls to discuss their careers and gauge their interest in helping a law student who is interested in pursuing the area of law they practice (i.e., me).

For me, this was a great approach to networking for multiple reasons. It was much less daunting than having to meet someone in person just to find out whether they have any interest in helping you. I could take the alumni list, research their professional backgrounds and experience, and choose to reach out or not reach out to them via an introductory email. One benefit of email is that it allows you to say what you want to say in a carefully crafted and nuanced way. And, often, a career counselor will be willing to review an email before you send it and give you feedback that not only helps you to improve the initial email but also allows you to consider future responses to follow-up questions you might receive in reply.

What to Prepare

Email correspondence with individuals in your network often leads to phone calls or one-on-one coffee meetings, which are good next steps for a few reasons. First, a phone call or in-person meeting is an opportunity to get to know someone who may be able to advocate on your behalf at their own place of work or at another firm. Second, it is an opportunity to develop the quality of your network. The more you interact with someone, the more that relationship develops. Ideally, networking relationships are not purely transactional. If a network connection is inviting you out for coffee or requesting a phone call, take them up on it.

Naturally, a phone call is easier to prepare for than an in-person meeting, and it's also a lower pressure scenario. During a phone call, you can have your resume and other notes in front of you, including a list of questions or comments that you can raise during the conversation. *Also, speaking from personal experience, if there is an awkward silence, that silence is never as awkward over the phone as it is when you're face-to-face with someone.* Furthermore, speaking over the phone can make it easier to speak authentically about yourself and the type of job you are looking for because you don't have to worry about things like whether you look too nervous or have something in your teeth.

Even though it may be "just" a phone call, timeliness is just as important as it is with in-person meetings. Being on time is the first step to making a good impression. It shows the other person that you value their time. It is always a good idea to reach out to the other person in advance to confirm who will call whom. In my experience, the other person is likely to want to call you if the call is taking place during normal work hours. *Woohoo! One less thing to worry about. (But make sure on the day of your phone call that your phone is not on silent and that your ringtone volume is all the way up.)* If for some reason you are going to be late or need to cancel, the other person know right away and give them some context or an explanation. Ask if they are still willing to connect at another time. *If you do this and they are willing to reschedule, make sure that you actually follow through and set up a new time.*

Nowadays, video messaging and video conferencing are popular modes of communication. Zoom meetings and the like are common alternatives to the traditional phone call. You can keep your notes and your resume in front of you just as you would during a phone call with one caveat: *Make sure that they are not in front of your camera where the other person can see them.*

Additionally, you will want to make sure that you are in a quiet location with a plain background. Having a Zoom call in a coffee shop or other public location can be risky. Background noise can make it so that the person you are speaking with can't hear you clearly or maybe can't hear you at all. *If you find yourself in this situation, be sure to apologize up front and explain why you had to choose the noisy location.* Also—dress professionally, not semi-formally. Dress for the job you want, not the job you have. *This piece of advice comes directly from personal experience—I once had a first-round interview in which the interviewer told me to wear a tie for the second round. So embarrassing!* As someone who felt insecure whenever I didn't already have an internship or job lined up, putting on a suit and tie always gave me a pre-meeting boost of confidence. (That one time when I didn't wear a tie, I was currently employed and was interviewing for a new role. I had become too complacent. But more on that later....)

The next step following a call or video chat is to meet that person in real life. *This is starting to sound like an online dating app—first communicate in writing, then over phone and video, and then finally, in person! Will there be any chemistry?!* If the thought of an in-person meeting gives you anxiety, here are some tips to help make it more bearable. First, if you have already connected with them via phone or Zoom, then you can take it as a good sign that they are willing to meet in person. That's because their time is valuable. If they did not think it would be productive to meet you in person, they wouldn't meet you.

Having an in-person networking meeting can be more difficult than a call or video meeting because your resume and notes might not be right in front of you. And, even if they are accessible, you should be making eye contact with the person you are speaking with, and not staring at your papers. With that said, you should definitely bring your resume with you: Maybe the other person wants a copy, or maybe you want to ask them whether they would give feedback or recommendations based on your resume. And don't forget to prepare questions in advance of any in-person networking meetings. Sure, you can write down questions and take them with you, but your goal should be to integrate them into your conversation without having to refer to your notes constantly. Remember, the purpose of these meetings is to *build a relationship*. Talking about issues involving legal practice or law school is important, but sharing information about yourself and your interests and learning about the other person's interests and legal experiences is just as important. Making connections is an important part of being a human. Make the most of the process.

Find Your Russ

I was able to practice one-on-one networking by signing up for the LGBT Bar Association of New York mentoring program. This program matches law students with more seasoned attorneys based on areas of interest. I had filled out an information sheet and stated that I was interested in LGBTQ+ advocacy law and real property law and ended up being matched with a mentor named Russ. Russ was the ideal mentor: a confident lawyer, friendly, and genuinely interested in what my interests were and how he could help me to expand my career search. I was extremely lucky to have been paired up with him. I had the same conversation with him that I had with my career counselor—about my interests in international, LGBTQ+, and real property law. He, too, thought that real property law would be a great area of law to start out in and that it would allow me to pivot into another area more easily if I decided to change fields. But Russ's help did not stop there. He was quick to invite me to attend networking events sponsored by the LGBT Bar Association of New York and to introduce me to co-workers and others in his network who could help me to practice my interviewing skills. And he continued to check in with me to see how my job search and bar prep were going.

But not all networking opportunities are going to arise according to the above pattern. Not all one-on-one in-person meetings are preceded by a series of emails or calls, and many networking opportunities arise from large group gatherings. This latter category in particular can be quite intimidating. The idea of walking into a room full of lawyers, not knowing anyone, and trying to learn about people's careers and experiences without coming off as too timid or meek can be scary. But here again, proper preparation is the key to success.

Begin by asking yourself the following: What is the purpose of the networking event? Is it for bankruptcy lawyers? Is it for LGBTQ lawyers? Is it to celebrate an event in someone's honor? Is it a legal education panel? Once you know the event's purpose, you can do research on the relevant type of law. Maybe you can even find a guest list and use that to get a better idea about the areas of law that will be represented at the event. You can then use this information to prepare questions or talking points that attendees may be interested in hearing about.

But of all the things you might do to make such events feel less daunting, attending them with one or more friends might be the most effective.

I'll never forget my first major networking event in Manhattan. I wore a blue suit, a white button-up, and a floral tie. *And I was nervous sweating so much that I thought about just going home.* The closer I got to the fancy New York City Law Firm that was hosting a LGBTQ+ pride networking event for lawyers, the slower and slower I walked, hoping to just come to a complete stop and miss the entire event. I entered the building and took an elevator up to one of the top floors. When the doors opened, I stepped out into what appeared to be an endless sea of lawyers chatting with one another, moving from group to group. *Is this hell? No, focus, focus, this is good for you.* But before I could turn around and leave, I spotted Russ picking up his nametag. I went over to say hello to him and pick up mine as well. As he had in the past, he quickly introduced me to other lawyers he knew. I was still nervous, but I wasn't feeling overwhelmed anymore. Most of the experienced lawyers I spoke with that day were very receptive to my questions about their careers. They shared personal experiences about the state of the legal field back when they graduated from law school and how they got to their current role. At the end of each conversation, they gave me their business cards and I gave them mine. (*Thanks, Staples!*) Thanks to Russ's support, I was able to meet other lawyers and make new networking connections without any awkwardness.

At some point, you will have to attend a networking event solo. But there are still actions you can take to make things easier for yourself: research the event, set goals for yourself, and RSVP "yes."

Research the event: I touched on this above. Researching the event itself can help you in developing a set of questions that you can use in your conversations with other attendees or speakers. (And if you can find the event's guest list online, you may see some names you recognize—if you reach out to them, you might not have to attend the event alone after all!)

Set clear goals: Your goals for these events can be anything. Maybe your goal is to share your business card with three other people. Maybe it is to not only attend a panel but ask the speakers a question. Whatever the goal, it should be designed to make the most of the networking event. If you are the type of person who gets nervous at networking events, setting clear goals can bring additional benefits. Once you have met your goals for the day/evening, you not only can leave, but can leave with a feeling of accomplishment.

RSVP "yes": The act of RSVPing "yes" is more powerful than you might think. Once an event is added to your calendar, it becomes real. You are more likely to commit to it. And you are more likely to prepare for it and set goals for yourself. So often, people overthink these events and then they don't actually show up when the day finally arrives. RSVPing "yes" and putting it on your calendar is one way to avoid this tendency.

My Big Break

After studying for and taking the bar exam, Russ encouraged me to try to set up a meeting with a family friend I previously interned for at a real estate law firm. After being unable to find a day or time that worked for both of us, I began to think that we wouldn't be meeting up any time soon.

"Our email exchanges just kind of ended without anything being set up. Should I just reach out to her and ask to set up a phone call again? Or should I try to see her in person?"

Am I being annoying? I don't think this firm even hires recent graduates. Do I really want to do this?

"Well, if she's tried to coordinate a meeting with you, it's not like she doesn't want to see you. Here's an idea: send her a new email letting her know that you're meeting some friends for dinner by her office and that you'd love to stop by if she's free. That way you offer a day and time that works for you to meet up with her, and then even if she isn't available, you're putting yourself back on her radar to set up a call or meeting for another time."

Russ, you are a genius! I'll give it a shot.

I did just as Russ suggested, and sure enough, my family friend ended up being free that night. I was able to stop by, catch up with her, and tell her that the bar exam was behind me and that I was currently looking for a job in real estate. She confirmed that her firm does not hire recent law school graduates; however, her friend's law firm does, and she would reach out to him on my behalf. I thanked her for her time and said I'd better go meet my friends for dinner. *I went home.*

Little did I know at the time, but that conversation would lead to my first interview for a real estate attorney position at my family friend's law firm a few weeks later.

> *Hi John,*
>
> *I have some good news for you: we're looking to hire two new law school grads. I already sent your resume to the hiring manager. Let her know when you're free for an interview.*

I was never so excited or relieved to receive an email. We scheduled an interview for the next week, and I began preparing.

Having finished the bar exam and being *extremely, extremely* unemployed, I had ample time to prepare for this interview. I broke down my tasks into a few different areas: my resume, real estate law, the law firm itself, the people I would be interviewing with, and general interview questions.

At the time, most of my experience was in the form of legal internships, both during and before law school. My most relevant experience was a pre-law school internship at this same real estate firm, and so I placed it front and center on my resume. I memorized that portion of my resume, making sure that I could thoroughly explain my role and the various tasks I had performed. I made sure that I could explain what I found interesting about each task and how it all motivated to learn more about the area of law. I then repeated the same process for the rest of the internships listed on my resume. Because I was a recent law school graduate, I made a point of highlighting past leadership positions, the different scholarships I received and why I received them, and the interests I explored during law school.

Next, I focused on crafting a compelling story to explain why I was interested in this position. I googled various topics in real estate law. I reflected on my personal experiences during my internship at this law firm. I remember thinking that playing a role in real estate deals was exciting. I enjoyed the fast pace and having to think on your feet to help the client achieve their goals. Since I had previously interned at this firm, I already had an idea of what I could expect. I also conducted online searches for different New York real estate laws to get an idea of the changes taking place in this area of the law and to familiarize myself with them on a basic level.

I then familiarized myself with the law firm and the people I would be interviewing with. At the time, the law firm did not have a website, but I used my previous internship experience to deduce that this was a medium-sized law firm that focused on real estate law but also had a few smaller areas of practice. I looked up the LinkedIn profiles of the hiring manager and of the managing partner who would be interviewing me. I could see how long they had been at the law firm, where they went to law school, and how their career paths developed. Researching the individuals who will be interviewing you can help you to identify similarities or connections (e.g., same law school, similar volunteer work) that you can then bring up during the interview. Working these commonalities into your conversation with the interviewer can help to build rapport between the interviewer and yourself.

Last but not least, I searched online for general law interview questions and then put them into an Excel spreadsheet. What is your biggest strength? *I work so hard and never stop working until the job gets done! Control-Alt-Delete. My biggest strength is my organizational skills. I keep a detailed agenda and it allows me to get work done on time and I make sure no task, big or small, falls through the cracks.* What is your biggest weakness? *I don't have any! Control-Alt-Delete. My biggest weakness is that sometimes I don't ask for help when I need it, and then I end up wasting time.* Why do you want this job? *I need money to pay back my student loans. Control-Alt-Delete. I'm eager to build my career among some of the best and brightest in the industry. I want to learn from and contribute to a strong team.* Why should we hire you instead of anyone else? *I do a great Jennifer Coolidge impersonation. Control-Alt-Delete. My previous experience at this firm, my go-getter attitude, and my successes from law school help make me the right fit for this team.*

My interview was broken up into two parts. I interviewed with two partners before interviewing with the managing partner. My interview with the two partners went well. Most of their questions were of the general, law-based kind. They asked about my previous internship at the firm, why I wanted to join full time, and why I should be hired. They asked about my 1L summer internship at the United Nations. Things must have gone well because they let me know that an interview with the managing partner would be forthcoming.

A few days later, I was back at the firm for the final step of the interview process. It was toward the end of the day. I was brought into the big conference room outside of the managing partner's office. There was a wooden table with a few desk chairs on each side of it. I nervously flipped through my resume and prepared my talking points. A few minutes later the managing partner walked in. He was wearing beautifully pressed pants, a white button-up, and a perfectly knotted tie. It was the end of the day, and yet he was still perfectly put together, as if he had only just gotten dressed. *And there I was, trying not to sweat through my suit.* He quickly looked at my resume and asked why I was interested in coming back to the firm. I recited my prepared answer from memory, and he seemed pleased. He then began to explain how junior attorneys would arrive at the firm, work there for a year or two to get great experience, and then leave for other positions elsewhere. So now, he said, the firm was looking for some entry-level attorneys who would eventually want to become partners. Do you want to become a partner here? *Do I want to become a partner here? Is the pope Catholic? Of course I want to become a partner here.* I could feel my pupils dilate with joy at the thought of that career path. *Today I'm just interviewing at this firm, but one day I can become a partner here.*

In hindsight, the comment about multiple junior attorneys' leaving after a year or two should have been a red flag. But at the time, I was so enthralled at the thought of becoming a partner that I doubled down on my interest and commitment to the firm and explained how eager I was to obtain the position.

A few days later, the email I was hoping for finally hit my inbox: *We'd like to offer you an associate attorney position at the firm.*

In that moment, I felt my dreams becoming reality. All the hard work I had put into law school and the bar exam had suddenly paid off.

Little did I know how many curve balls were just around the corner.

5

Your First Job Out of Law School (Will Hopefully Be Better Than Mine)

I swirled my iced coffee as I stood on the N train and counted the stops until I finally entered Manhattan. It was my first day as a lawyer, and if the giant smile and giddy pep in my step did not give it away, I do not know what would: I was thrilled.

Once I reached the office, the admins at the front desk called over the hiring partner. She introduced me to a few of the other lawyers who arrived at work early that day and then brought me to my desk. It was an old but solid wooden desk in a shared office with two other junior attorneys. One had been at the firm for a few months but was on vacation for the week, and the other would be starting after me. *First week and I have the office to myself. Nice!*

I set up my computer and waited for work to be sent my way.

In the weeks that followed, I would meet my two office mates (who were great!) and a number of other attorneys. During my internship, I had worked with two associate attorneys, but they had left the firm by time I joined (*insert ominous foreshadowing here*), so I was basically meeting everyone for the first time. As more attorneys learned that the firm had hired two new associates tasks, we started to receive more assignments. Different attorneys needed different types of help depending on the type of deal they were working on. As the majority of my prior experience involved working on closing statements, I was excited to learn about the other parts of real estate transactions. However, not much learning occurred.

The Bullying and Incivility Become Apparent

When I was hired, there was no organizational chart mapping out the firm's hierarchy. It was not clear who reported to whom. *I was never even given a direct supervisor or manager.* There was the managing partner, partners, associates, and me, the new guy at the bottom of the totem pole. I began to receive assignments from many of these attorneys. I'd receive the assignments via a brief email or quick conversation along with a few documents and a file folder—but not many instructions. So I would read through the documents, compile a list of questions, and complete the parts of the assignments I understood before following up with the attorney who assigned the project. But, more often than not, that attorney would be busy with other work, so they'd ask me to come by later or send me to another associate attorney who could explain things to me. Sometimes, those associate attorneys would have time to explain things thoroughly, but often, their explanations had to be rushed to make time for other obligations. More often than not, I was left by myself with outstanding work and no idea how to get started. The whole situation was inefficient and anxiety-inducing.

This was a jarring experience for me, as I had always been a "box checker" when it came to all things school and work. I was not used to producing incomplete work or, worse, taking on a project and making things much worse than they had been. Reaching the same dead end on multiple projects brought on a sense of dread that I had never before experienced. As the anxiety built up, the negative self-talk in my head became louder and louder. *What are you doing? Do you even understand any of this? You are going to get fired. Do you even want to practice real estate law? What are you doing here?*

This anxiety was exacerbated by the negative social interactions that I began to experience. There was a lot of work to get done and not enough people to do the work. Naturally, that led to a stressed out and anxious team. Lashing out was commonplace. Being a new attorney at the firm, *or a new attorney just in general,* did not shelter me from others' wrath.

As time went on, I was talked down to and yelled at. Once, I had been assigned to support a project in the litigation department. Compared to other attorneys I had encountered at the firm, the partner I was working with on this project was generally kind. *Okay, I thought to myself, maybe not everyone here is so bad.*

It was the Wednesday before the Thanksgiving holiday. That morning, an email had gone out: anyone who had completed their tasks for the day could leave at 2:00 p.m. The attorneys on the real estate transaction floor laughed. They knew that none of them would be leaving early.

I spent my lunch hour that day working on the litigation project and preparing my questions for the litigation partner. When I finished, I walked down one floor and knocked on his door.

"Hey, do you have a few minutes to discuss some questions I have about the litigation project?"

"Are you f***ing kidding me? It's a quarter to two before a holiday and you think now is the time to ask me questions? Right before you leave?"

I was stunned. I did not know how to respond. A bunch of attorneys had just been joking about how no one was leaving early. Now I'm being scolded for trying to get work done.

"Sorry, I'll come back with it later."

I quickly made my way back to the stairwell and paused there for a few minutes to collect myself.

Take a few big deep breaths. It's okay. Maybe he just has to leave early today? You still have a few hours to go. Get it together. Get it together. Get it together.

I stopped in the bathroom and splashed some water on my face, trying to calm my raging anxiety. I went back to my desk and tried to begin working on another project, but I couldn't concentrate. All I could do was replay in my head what had just happened. *I'm not actually leaving at 2 p.m. Why didn't I say that to him? Should I have just waited until after the holiday? I'm not even on the litigation team. I'm just helping out!*

I tried to put it behind me, but little did I know that this would be just one of many incidents.

Another time, the managing partner asked me to request information from a title company. I took my draft and ran it by one of the senior associates. The senior associate gave me the green light, so I sent out the email request, cc'ing the managing partner. A few minutes later, the managing partner showed up at my office door. My two office-mates were present in the room.

"John, I saw the request that you sent out. It was *very obvious that you're a junior attorney* and that this was your first request. You didn't need to ask for all that information. You only need to request some of the basic information."

"Okay, thank you for the heads up. I'll only request the basic information next time."

Once the managing partner walked away, I put my head down and tried not to make eye contact with the two junior attorneys I shared an office with. *It's obvious that you're a junior attorney.* Those words kept ringing in my head. *What will these other junior attorneys think of me now? I'm so embarrassed. Did he have to announce it to everyone? Does the senior associate who helped me draft the request know this?*

The number of incidents grew over time. Partners would assign work to me and then tell me to get out of their office when I'd show up with questions. I would try to approach a senior associate with questions, only to be told that he cannot do his job and my job. I witnessed jarring interactions between partners and associate attorneys—one time, a partner threw papers at an associate attorney for not fixing a typo, and another time, a partner screamed at a senior associate in front of the whole floor for not formatting a document to her liking.

About a month into my new role, I had to take a day off to report to jury duty. *Thank God!* I had first been summoned months earlier, when I was still in law school, but had opted to postpone it. I didn't have a job lined up at the time, so I wasn't particularly concerned about whether I'd have to take time off from work. And yet here I was, taking a day off from work to attend jury duty.

Well, this is still better than missing class or study time for the bar exam. Having an extra day off during the week where I don't have to go into that godforsaken office is a blessing. Has anyone else ever considered jury duty a blessing? Just me?

I packed up my computer, chargers, and a padfolio containing a clean copy of my paper and a stack of printed-out articles and made my way to the downtown Brooklyn courthouse. *If I was going to spend time on jury duty, I might as well try to work on the paper I am trying to get published.* I waited in line, walked through the metal detector, and then followed signs to the jury waiting room. It was a giant room filled with rows of gray seats. At the front of the room stood a podium, and behind the podium, a court clerk who called up potential jurors and directed them to different courtrooms. I sat down, filled out my jury duty card, and then scrolled through the usual apps on my phone. *Email. LinkedIn. Instagram. Facebook. Twitter. Repeat. Repeat. Repeat.* Eventually, I stopped refreshing my apps, opened up my padfolio, picked up a pen, and began to reread my article.

Before now, I thought this article was in good shape. However, as I sat there rereading it, the comments, strikeouts, and arrows flowing from my colored pens indicated otherwise. I became totally enthralled in the editing process. It was as if time stopped and I was alone in that waiting room. Cutting down wordy sentences, adding relevant sources to new sections, double-checking footnotes—I was loving it all.

This is so much fun! I love this!

Editing my article felt natural. It brought me a sense of joy in my work that I hadn't felt in what seemed like eons. It was as if there were puzzle pieces in front of me coming together, piece by piece. I could start to see the full, beautiful image and was excited to see this project through.

But this elation did not last long.

Today I get to edit my article but tomorrow morning, bright and early, it's back to the grind of the office.

That warm feeling of joy dissipated, replaced by a cold, endless pit of despair. It was jarring how rapidly I went from feeling calm and content to jittery and anxious.

Why am I going back to something that I hate doing when I know there's something else I love so much? There has to be something else out there I can do. Something with more reading and writing and editing. I can't keep doing this forever. I'm on the wrong path. Oh God. I am on the wrong path.

Yet this experience was not the straw that broke the camel's back (*crying next to Elmo in Times Square was... more ominous foreshadowing*).

I felt as though I was trapped in a job I hated, with no way out. I worried that I made the wrong choice and would never have the chance to pursue better options. I would carry this feeling with me for months as I tried to find my place in the legal industry. The stark contrast I felt between doing work I was passionate about and work I hated was branded into my brain. That wound is no longer fresh, but the scar remains.

Shortly after experiencing this professional identity crisis, my name was called. I was being summoned to a criminal courtroom for jury selection. A judge introduced us potential jurors to the prosecution and the defense. One of the prosecutors was a buddy from high school's older brother.

"Does anyone here have a reason why they cannot serve on a jury?" The judge asked.

Before I could stand up and say that I was friends with the prosecutor's brother, another man stood up. He said it was against his religious beliefs to convict someone and sentence them to prison.

"No worries, sir, we'll send you back downstairs so you can sit on a civil trial instead. *They are MUCH longer than criminal trials,*" the judge hissed. "Anyone else?"

I slowly stood up, fearing that I would get similarly scolded.

"I know the prosecutor's brother. We're friends from high school." I stated the name of my friend, the name of my high school, and my class year. The prosecutor's brother gave me a wave and confirmed with the judge that this was all true information.

"Okay, thank you for sharing. You can still stay here for questions."

Ah, shit. I might be on the jury now. Actually wait... maybe that's not such a bad thing. Oh. Hold on. What if I can get on a civil trial? Those are longer.

These ideas volleyed back and forth in my mind as I tried to decide whether I wanted to be selected or not. The judge asked everyone a few questions before we broke for an hour-long lunch period.

As I was scarfing down a sandwich around the corner from the courthouse, in walked some young prosecutors, including one of my law school friends, Tony.

"Hey, John, how's it going? What are you doing here?"

"Here for jury duty! Have to head back in a half hour or so."

"Cool! We need to catch up one of these days."

"Definitely!"

Tony and his coworkers grabbed their sandwiches and left. I felt the knots in my stomach tighten. I wished that I had fun, young co-workers I could get lunch with. I finished up my lunch and headed back to the courtroom.

The judge let 6 of the 24 potential jurors know they were being summoned to sit for this trial. The other 18, myself included, were sent back to the jury waiting room, where we could be selected for a different trial. *Maybe even a civil trial! I could dream, right?*

Once back in the waiting room, I plopped down in an open seat and resumed editing. But before I knew it, the clerk announced that we were free to leave the courthouse.

I packed my bag and headed for the R train. As I walked, all sorts of thoughts filled my head: *Wow. I could work on my article forever! Ugh, but I have to wake up tomorrow and go back to the office.* My heart sank into my stomach. *I am so unhappy at the firm.* The thoughts kept coming. *Can I really keep going back to this job? Am I in the right place? Is it going to get better? Could it get worse?*

On a day where I didn't have to go to work, it sure feels like I got a lot done.

The R train pulled into the station. I did not feel like jumping in front of it.

The stress of feeling trapped in an unsupportive work environment started to take a toll on my mental and physical health. After my jury duty revelation, every weeknight and weekend, all I did was think about how I was how fast the next workday was approaching and I was going to get through it. I could not stop thinking about how this was the wrong job for me. This was not how I wanted to build my career.

After about six weeks of keeping these feelings to myself, I began to have conversations with my partner and my parents about leaving the real estate firm. My partner was very understanding and supportive from the get-go. My parents were as well, but they felt that I should try to stick it out for a little while longer and that I find another job before resigning.

During my lunch breaks, I began to reach out to my career counselor from law school and other networking connections. I scoured numerous job sites and portals. I became so desperate to find a new job that I would have accepted almost anything just to leave this toxic work environment.

With each passing day, my anxiety became more consuming. I could feel it in my throat. I had to take deep breaths throughout the workday and just try to fight through it. By my seventh or eighth week on the job, I started using my lunch hour as a means of escape. I'd scarf down some food and then just walk around Manhattan, dreading the thought returning to that office.

On December 18th, 2019, I finally reached my breaking point. Right before lunch, a partner yelled at me for not completing a project to her liking, one that she had not explained how to complete. Afterward, I quickly ran out of the building for lunch and started walking around. But when it was time to return to the office, I couldn't. I felt tears welling up. So instead of going back to work, I walked into Times Square and stopped under the awning of a skyscraper. As hundreds of tourists walked past me, looking up at the buildings ooh-ing and ahh-ing, I took out my phone and called my mom.

"Mom," I said, with a cracking voice and tears streaming down my face.

"Aw, my son, what's wrong?"

"I'm just having a really bad day." The tears turned into sobs.

"I can't go back into that office one more time. I can't. I can't. I can't."

"It's okay, it's going to be okay. Take some deep breaths. We all have bad days sometimes. It's part of life. Take some deep breaths."

The more she told me it was okay, the harder I sobbed. It was at this point that someone dressed up as Elmo, who had been taking photos with tourists in Times Square, came and stood next to me as I was sobbing on the phone with my mom. He removed his

Elmo head and took a few sips of water. I briefly made eye contact with him as I took a few deep breaths. He looked at me with pity. I sobbed harder.

"I can't go back in. I can't do it. I'm quitting. I'm quitting. I'm quitting."

"Okay, it's okay. If you need to quit, you need to quit. It's okay. I think you should try to hang in there until you find something else, but if the job is going to leave you like this, it's okay."

"Okay, after work today, I'm drafting my resignation letter, and tomorrow, I'm handing it in."

"Do it. You need to. You can finish up today, give your two weeks' notice, and then it will be behind you."

For the first time in weeks, I felt relief. I wiped my eyes, kept my head down as I walked past Elmo who was now on his break, and took another lap around the block before returning to the office. My first legal job after law school was coming to an end rather quickly.

The next day, I showed up to work with resignation letter in hand. It was short and brief. In it, I thanked the managing partner for the opportunity, stated that the role was not for me, and gave my two weeks' notice. After settling in at my desk, I walked to the managing partner's office and asked his admin if he was free. He was not in yet, so I'd have to try again later. Eager to get this over with, I continued to check back in. On my fourth attempt, success. I walked in with my resignation letter and handed it to him. My voice shook as I thanked him for the opportunity and offered my two weeks' notice. I could hardly believe that I was finally saying these words. In a monotonous tone, he said he was sorry to see me go and that he understood that this role is not for everyone. He then handed the letter back and told me to give it to the office manager.

Afterward, I went back to my desk and stared blankly at my screen. I mostly felt relief, but sadness and disappointment were there, too. I also felt some anxiety about having to tell the family friend who worked at the firm that I had resigned so soon. I decided to wait until the next day to tell her. And then the next day. And the next. Finally, about a week later, I told her. I walked into her office and, with a shaking voice, asked her if she had a minute. She told me to take a seat and that no matter what I was about to say, she would not be disappointed in me. *Oh God, she already knows. What a shame that she couldn't hear it from me first.* With my voice still shaking, I explained that I was leaving and why. Like the managing partner, she told me that she understood and that this high-pressure role is not for everyone. But she also told me not to be so hard on myself and to find something that I am interested in and will enjoy doing.

I had finally ripped off all the band-aids that needed to be ripped off. I would just need to make it through one more week...or so I thought. Toward the end of the day, I received an email stating that I was not needed for one more week but rather only two more days. *Thank God! You don't need to tell me twice. That sounds good to me.*

When my last day finally arrived I could not contain my excitement. I started packing right after I got in and began to make a list of all the projects and deals that needed to be assigned to other attorneys. As I was doing this, the hiring partner, the IT analyst, and a young man about my age walked into the office.

"Oh, you're still here?" asked the hiring partner.

"Yup, today is my last day."

"Oh, we thought yesterday was your last day. This is the new hire who will be taking over your position. We actually need to set him up at your desk."

The hiring partner peeked out into the admins' cubicles and found an empty desk.

"You can work out of this desk for today."

"Sure thing, sounds good to me."

I took my belongings to one of the admin's cubicles and finished up making my list of projects to pass off and put documents together for each project.

That afternoon, the new attorney approached my desk with a few questions.

"Sorry to hear it's my first day and your last day. Leaving for a new position?"

"Yeah, me too. And yes, I am."

"What's your next role?"

"Not sure yet, still figuring it out."

"Oh, okay. Well, would you mind if I asked you a few questions before you leave?"

"Yeah, sure thing."

"Okay, I guess to start, who is my manager?"

"I don't know. I kind of just had attorneys coming up to me and giving me things to work on, so kind of everyone."

"Wait... you don't have a manager?"

"Nope."

"Well who should I ask to figure this out?"

"I'm really not sure."

"I'll let you finish up what you're working on then and figure it out myself."

I could see the aggravated expression on his face. I felt sorry for him. *I wish I could say "Run! Run while you still can!"*

At the end of the day, I said my goodbyes, handed in my ID card, and walked out the building's revolving door for the last time. I felt like a person who had finished serving a prison sentence. I was free. Even though I knew I was about to be facing the stress of searching for a new job, in that moment, I didn't care. I felt as though the weight of the world had been lifted off my shoulders. I made it out alive.

6

Networking for a Job Part 2 (The Meantime?)

I was back at square one. Within a few days of quitting, the temporary high of freedom had faded and panic began to set in. I didn't know what was next.

I was back to scouring legal job portals, refreshing these sites every few hours, hoping for anything. *Insurance attorney? Sure! Staff attorney at a family law clinic? I'll give it a shot! Immigration attorney? Let's do it.* In my shame and panic, I was casting the widest net possible. How could I have quit my first job as a lawyer? Was I cut out for this? Should I do something else? The uncertainty weighed on me heavily, and I wanted an answer.

Days turned into weeks. Applying for jobs day in and day out made every day seem like Groundhog Day. I told very few people that I was looking for a new job. The shame of being an unemployed lawyer was eating me alive. I was praying for any job offer whatsoever.

One day I came across a new online job posting for a compliance position at Société Générale. *Looking for a recent law school grad, good critical thinking skills, strong working ethic. Okay, I might be qualified for this.* I sent in my resume and began doing some research on the company. I discovered that I was connected to someone on LinkedIn who worked there: a former law school classmate, Eric. Eric was the Student Bar Association Treasurer at Brooklyn

Law School when I was the LGBT Organization's Treasurer. During my 2L year, I had to appeal my budget proposal before him and ask (*beg*) for more money. We ended up getting some extra funding (*thank you, Eric*), but apart from that interaction and a few passing conversations, I did not know him particularly well. I checked out his LinkedIn page and debated whether I should reach out to him.

I don't know him too well, so this message might be weird. What if he doesn't respond? What if he tells everyone I'm an unemployed loser?! But on the other hand, what do I have to lose at this point? I am an unemployed loser!

I sent him a generic message asking whether he liked working at Société Générale and if he had any advice about applying for a compliance job there. He responded right away, sharing his phone number and telling me that I could text or call him with any questions. He also told me there was an open sanctions compliance internship position on his team and that I would be a great fit for it. He had held the role previously and felt that it had been a great steppingstone on his path to becoming a sanctions compliance associate. I let him know that I was extremely interested in the position and sent him my resume to pass on to his manager.

I spent the next few weeks applying for new jobs, going on the occasional interview, and incessantly checking my inbox. Eventually, I received the news that I had been offered an interview for the compliance role at Société Générale. I let Eric know, and he filled me in on the interview process there. He also let me know that the role on his team was still being processed and still open.

To prepare for my interview, I repeated all the usual steps: I did lots of research on the company, brushed up on the compliance industry, took notes, prepared sample interview questions to practice with, and identified some personal highlights that I wanted to weave into my interview answers. *Working at the real estate law firm was not included in these highlights!* By the time I showed up for my interview, I was well prepared, eager to work, and nervous!

At Société Générale, I was interviewed by three different compliance managers. I had been crossing my fingers that no one would ask me about why my tenure at the real estate law firm had been so short-lived, and fortunately no one did. *What's a good way of saying everyone was miserable, I wasn't supported in any of the work that I did, and I wanted to throw myself in front of the R train*? However, the last interviewer did ask me to give one example of something I liked and something I did not like about a previous job.

"Well, one aspect of my previous job that I liked was being able to work on different closing statements for different deals. As for one aspect of my previous job that I did not like, I have to think about that for a moment...."

I probably paused for a good 20 or 30 seconds.

Well I can't say that I didn't really like everything else about the job. How can I sugarcoat this?

"Well, one aspect of my previous job that I did not like was working on projects that were more administrative than legal and required a lot of tedious efforts. It was not very interesting to me."

Right away I could see a frown come across the interviewer's face.

"Well," he said, "I can tell you with this job not every task will be an interesting one. There are actually quite a few administrative tasks that we all take part in to help keep the team afloat."

Ah, damn it. Actually, can I go back and change my answer? I'll just let you know that the previous work and people were not my cup of tea and I'm looking to do something different.

"Oh I understand," I said, trying to recover. "I'm a team player and committed to doing what needs to be done in order to keep the team running like a well-oiled machine. I am just always eager for new work and opportunities."

His demeanor did not change. I could tell that this last question may have sunk my chances of obtaining this job.

Over the next few days, while I anxiously awaited a response for this compliance position, I received another email from Société Générale—for the open position on Eric's team. I excitedly texted Eric to let him know and to ask whether he had any advice about his team specifically. He suggested a few websites to help me brush up on my sanctions knowledge and assured me that the interviewers were really good people who were eager to build a strong and effective team. When I arrived at the building on the day of my interview, Eric came downstairs to greet me in the lobby. We hadn't seen each other in person since he graduated from law school, but we greeted each other as if no time had passed it all. He then accompanied me to back up to his floor where my three interviews would be taking place.

My answers for these interviews came much more naturally than they did when I was interviewing for the compliance role. Thankfully, none of these interviewers asked me what my favorite and least favorite aspects of my previous job were (though I had come prepared to answer such a question this time).

After the interviews were over, Eric met up with me again and briefly introduced me to some of the team that he was working with. I told him that I would keep him posted and that I would accept the role on the spot if I received an offer.

A few days later, *which felt like years to me, an unemployed person,* I finally received the email I was hoping for: "We would like to extend you an offer for the position on the sanctions compliance team at Société Générale." *Finally. Finally!* I let out a giant exhale. After accepting the role, it took about five or six weeks for me to get my start date, and then the countdown was on!

Finally, on February 24, 2020, I began my first day at Société Genérale as a sanctions compliance intern.

Take two. Here we go. . . .

7

Does This Count as My First or Second Job Out of Law School?

Beginning my job at Société Générale was very different from beginning my job at the real estate law firm for a few major reasons. First, because I had a genuine interest in this field, I cared about learning more and growing in it, which was an exciting change of pace for me. Second, I really hit it off with the people I was working with. I felt comfortable speaking with my manager and asking him questions, and I was on a team with six other people who were all open to answering my questions. This emphasis on group work made me feel like I was part of the team instead of a loner trying to survive. Third, after working in the office for only three weeks, the COVID-19 pandemic hit, forcing me to work from home for a year and a half.

Given the physical restrictions that were put in place during the pandemic, clear communication with management and team members became paramount. Part of my role as a sanctions compliance intern involved screening incoming transactions for possible sanctions nexuses and dispositioning them accordingly. Before the pandemic hit, I could pull up a chair next to my colleagues who also performed this work and train alongside them, face to face. After the pandemic hit, I lost this luxury. Instead of greeting everyone in the morning or getting lunch with the team in the middle of the day, I was reduced to a name on our Skype list. Easy to be forgotten.

My interactions with the team decreased significantly during those first few weeks.

"We'll only be working remotely for two weeks," the C Suite advised.

Two weeks later, we were given the same message. Then again two weeks after that. It eventually became apparent that we would not be returning anytime soon.

Despite this curveball, I still wanted to be successful in this role and prove that I was worthy of being on the team. I wanted to prove that they hired the right person. Fortunately, I felt comfortable enough to reach out to Eric for help. By the time I was hired, he had already been on the team for about a year and a half and so was very knowledgeable about the sanctions field. He continued to teach me the screening methods the team used and encouraged me to ping or call colleagues who could also show me the ropes or offer advice. Because of his guidance, I went from being shy about, embarrassed about, or reluctant to reach out to others for help to being confident enough to speak up when I wasn't sure about something. *What a difference from my former job!*

Although I wasn't necessarily prepared for remote work, I was nevertheless able to find some silver linings and use this new setup to my advantage. Having to heavily rely on Skype to communicate with colleagues was one of these silver linings. I liked how Skype showed me whether someone was available, away, or busy. In instances where people were available, I knew I had the green light to reach out to them. This, to me, was preferable to the uncertainty of initiating interactions in the real world. I also liked that I could draft and edit what I wanted to say versus coming up with something on the spot during a real-life conversation. I eventually developed my own voice, a friendly and cheerful communication style, and built up confidence through the use of instant messaging.

Gaining the confidence to ask questions openly and freely was vital to my success in this position. I knew I had a supportive team that was willing to educate me. Learning to accept that I did not have all the answers and knowing that I would not be scolded for asking questions allowed me to grow professionally and become a better sanctions subject-matter expert.

Having a genuine interest in the sanctions field helped to propel me forward in my role as a sanctions compliance intern. Because of my academic background (I had taken international law classes during law school and had an undergraduate degree in political science (and Spanish)), I already had some familiarity with the sanctions space and wanted to expand my knowledge. This base knowledge was a nice foundation upon which to grow my expertise. Slowly but surely I was able to contribute more and more to the team. I would send out relevant news articles and updates, work on different transaction-related questions, and perform research on issues that were facing the team. It was deeply gratifying for me to excel in a role after failing in my previous one.

As a newly hired intern, I was not 100 percent up to speed on how things worked, but I was given the tools to get there. The team helped to train me on the sanctions field generally and on the specific responsibilities of our team. Different team members would run hypothetical sanctions issues by me, I would offer my advice, and they would give me feedback and guidance for improving my answers. This helped to prepare me for eventually going "live," i.e., answering sanctions-related questions from other colleagues on other teams. I was encouraged to ask questions, continue learning, and develop my skill set. I was learning and improving every day, which gave me the confidence and motivation to keep moving forward.

Working with colleagues who wanted to train me and help me learn about the industry motivated me to continue learning on my own. Though I knew I could not do this work independently yet, I saw a path forward. I was excited because I knew that my efforts would help me become smarter and better at my job. Their eagerness to help me also made me determined to not let anyone down, including myself.

In the sanctions field, there is always something new to learn. I grew my knowledge by reading articles on my own time and staying abreast of sanctions news updates. The more knowledgeable

I became, the more I could contribute to the team. During my job search, I had read an article advising everyone to keep an inventory/running list of each new professional task and skill learned, and so I did. It's a useful exercise for updating your resume or for keeping track of just how far you've come and what you've learned. You might even be surprised by some of the more unexpected skills you've picked up.

"Hey John, I wanted to touch base with you on one last thing," my manager, Jay, said.

"Sure thing, how can I help you?"

"Well now that Dil will be leaving the team in the next month, we're going to need someone to take over handling the metrics for the team. Do you think you can throw some time on his calendar and start training with him so you can take over when he's gone?"

panics internally

"Yeah, sure thing. I'll touch base with him and get started with that. I'll let you know if any questions arise on my end."

"Thank you!"

When Jay asked me to help with the team's metrics, I was scared. I was only a few months in and still working to find my footing with my pre-existing responsibilities. I had no prior experience with the team metrics, but I handling them would add to my deliverables, and I had heard about how complicated it was to put it all together. I also was concerned that the person training me would be leaving the company within a month. *What if I had questions? What if I didn't know what to do?* I doubted whether I was the right person for this task.

My first training session didn't provide me with much comfort. As Dil explained all the different spreadsheets, PowerPoints, and online tools needed to find and organize the metrics, I remember feeling as if my heart would beat out of my chest. As he explained each deliverable in detail, I typed my notes and took screenshots as fast as I could.

"It's not that bad once you get the hang of it."

"Yeah, totally. I'm sure once you do it for a few months it starts to make sense," I said, trying to reassure myself that I could do it.

I met with Dil a few more times and did some metrics practice rounds. Doing some of the spreadsheets began to get easier, while others seemed to get harder. After each call, I'd add to my notes. But before I knew it, Dil was gone and the metrics were my responsibility. For the first month, whenever Jay would check in about the metrics, my heart would beat fast and my throat would close up.

"How are the metrics looking this month?"

"So far so good, I think. I'll keep you posted with a first draft and any questions I have soon."

Fortunately, Jay would review each spreadsheet before it was presented to upper-level management. I felt pressure to provide perfect responses on the first try, so before sending Jay a draft, I would read and reread each line of spreadsheet data and each word in my draft email. But I fell short of perfect on the first attempt many times.

"Some of the numbers in this section look too high. And some of the metrics in this section look too low. Can you rerun the numbers and tell me if anything changes?"

I would furiously read through my notes and recalculate the data.

Ah, he's right. This section is too high because I added an extra row of data to the calculation, and this section is too low because I added the missing row of data to the first section. Why am I so dumb?! How did I miss this? How did this one escape me even though I checked it at least five times?

These questions played on a loop in my head as I added the corrected spreadsheet to my email to Jay.

Hi Jay,

I looked into the sections you asked me about, and it turns out I'm an idiot. I added one row of data to a section it didn't belong in, and it messed everything up. I'm the worst!!! Sorry!!!!!

Control-Alt-Delete.

Hi Jay,

I took a look at the sections you pointed out. It turns out I accidentally added one row of data to the wrong section.

Once I added it to the right section, the new totals looked correct—they are more in line with the averages from the last few months. Apologies for the error. I'll be sure to double check this next month.

Best,

John

I feel the dread in my body, scratching at my chest from the inside. I'm so disappointed that I practiced so hard but still made a mistake on the metrics. Now I have to explain my careless error and hope that Jay understands. I pray it's not a big deal. But I'm prepared for the worst. I hit send.

I decide to switch to a different task and take a break from the metrics. But before I can even start, my inbox dings. There is a new email. And it's from Jay: "No worries. Thanks for the updated version."

That's not bad. I can work with that. I'm not getting fired. (At least I don't think I am.)

During that first month of handling the metrics, I felt good about what I could complete on my own and anxious about what I could not. I would sometimes meet with Jay and another colleague, Vanessa, to review some of the more complex metrics I had to put together. Every time I would set up a call with them, I'd feel anxiety course through my body, like waves of a reverberating, giant gong. But that anxiety would dissipate as they walked through answers to my questions or strategized about or came up with a game plan for issues that might arise down the line.

Also during that first month, I did many first, second, and third drafts. I was forced to get comfortable with the uncomfortable, which, for me, meant accepting that I would have lots of follow-up questions. And I slowly began to learn that asking for help (even if you have to do it multiple times) is okay. Both Jay and Vanessa had been at Société Générale for many years and were happy to share their knowledge with me. And, as they often said, taking the time to help me now would help them in the long run—once I could do the metrics independently, their lives would be easier.

When I submitted final metrics for the first time, I felt a combination of relief and pride: relief because I had submitted them on time and pride because I took on a challenge outside of my wheelhouse. I stepped up to the plate and helped my team out. (*Believe it or not, none of the lawyers I worked with were chomping at the bit to take on the team's metrics.*) I had searched for this feeling for so long. I was becoming a useful team player. It was a win under my belt.

After submitting the first month's metrics, I had about a week until I would have to start on metrics for the next month. I still made some mistakes and had questions, but there were fewer of both compared to the first month. And so it was with each subsequent month. Before I knew it, I didn't have anxiety about asking questions for the metrics. I even raised a few novel questions that helped to make the metrics stronger and more nuanced.

When I look back on this experience, I see a few lessons that can be applied to career development. One, even though you may be nervous or insecure, taking on new challenges is a great way to learn or develop new skills. Two, you are smarter and more adaptable than you think. In my case, I feared that the spreadsheets and PowerPoints would become too much for me to handle and so the project would end up being assigned to a more competent and intelligent colleague. But because I took my training seriously and asked the right questions, I eventually mastered the task assigned to me. Three, this experience exemplifies how a healthy team should operate. Though I had many, many questions for my colleagues, they were willing to spend time explaining a new process to me. They understood that helping me to become a metrics expert was beneficial not only for me, but also for them and the wider team. Four, this experience is a reminder not to let needless fear or anxiety get the best of us. I worried that every question I asked and draft I had to correct was a nail in my career's proverbial coffin. But being on a well functioning team meant that I was surrounded by colleagues who didn't want to see me fail. Rather, they encouraged me to ask questions and wanted to see me grow. And though I didn't realize it at the time, I would come to find out how valuable those metrics skills could be.

8

Side Hustles, Volunteering, and (More) Networking

Even after I began working at Société Genérale, in the back of my mind, the nagging questions persisted. Am I working in the field that I am truly passionate about? Honestly, I wasn't sure. Did I think the sanctions field was interesting? Sure. Did I want to do this forever? I didn't know. Did I at least want to do this in the short and medium term? Yes! A steady paycheck, benefits, and not wanting to throw myself in front of the R train every morning were all reasons to keep working and learning at Société Genérale. I was working from 9am to 6pm Mondays through Fridays, which left me ample time outside of work to explore potential side hustles and volunteering opportunities. During this time, I published a legal article, volunteered with the LGBT Bar Association of New York, and worked as a TA (and later adjunct professor) for pre-bar classes at Brooklyn Law School.

Publishing a Legal Article

Professor Marsha Garrison is a godsend. *And honestly, that is an understatement.* She is one of those professors who is always put together, weaves through complex legal issues effortlessly, and answers questions so well that you almost forget why you asked the question in the first place. I had the good fortune of being her student in Torts as a 1L and then again in Trusts and Estates as a 2L. When the time came to select fall classes as a 3L, I jumped at the chance to register for her seminar about the rule of law in Myanmar. (*Why was Brooklyn Law School offering a class on the rule of law in Myanmar? Great question!* Professor Garrison took a sabbatical in Myanmar, where she taught law classes and acquired a wealth of knowledge about the country and its legal system. She put together a seminar for Brooklyn Law students to share that knowledge with them. *All very casual, right?*)

Early on in the semester, during her office hours, I mentioned that I was interested in publishing a legal article.

"As a 2L, while I was writing my journal article, we were told that if we wrote about Kim Jung Un, it was unlikely that more than one of our articles would get published."

(I began writing my journal article in fall 2017. President Trump had already tweeted about Kim Jung Un multiple times, and lots of us 2Ls were eager to add our two cents.)

"But that is what I was the most interested in, so that's what I wrote about, and my article was understandably not chosen for publication. Now, looking back, I wish I was able to publish an article as a law student."

"You know, you still can."

Her succinct response has stuck with me. I've since applied this advice to other areas of life.

"Take the paper for this class, for instance. The page limit is only 15 pages, but you can revise it and add to it next semester as an independent study paper, and then shop it around to get it published."

I was stunned.

"Wow, that would be awesome! Could I work with you on this paper and get credit for independent study?"

"Of course. Let's talk about it and develop it more this semester, and then you can hit the ground running next semester."

When I walked into Professor Garrison's office hours that day, I had assumed that the opportunity to get published in a legal journal was behind me. Her words reassured me that just because you missed an opportunity in the past doesn't mean that you cannot seize all the new opportunities in front of you in the present.

That fall, I wrote a 15-page paper and created a PowerPoint presentation on the effect of British colonialism on LGBT criminal laws in Myanmar and India and how they had developed since the colonial period. The following semester, the final one of my law school career, I worked closely with Professor Garrison to find more resources, expand my ideas, and edit my paper, until I had a 35-page paper that was almost ready to be published.

"Take the summer to study for the bar, and take a break afterward. Once you start to get back into a routine in the fall, pick this paper back up and make your final edits. By then, it should be in good shape to shop around for publication."

Study for the bar exam, take a break, pick paper back up. Got it!

I was prepared to follow her advice to a T, but little did I know how crazy the fall would be. The next time I picked my paper back up would be that fateful day in the jury duty waiting room. But after that day, I continued to edit the paper during my spare time and kept in touch with Professor Garrison, who would offer me advice and review my revised drafts.

Once I had a final version, Professor Garrison helped guide me through the publishing process. I created a profile on the legal publishing website ExpressO and began to select the journals I would submit my work to. After choosing as many relevant journals as I could find (probably about 60 or so), I submitted my article and began the waiting game.

What if none of them wants to publish my article? Would this be a waste of time? Or, what if a lot of them want to publish it? How will I choose? How many times do I need to refresh this website before someone extends an offer to me?

After what felt like years (it was a few days), some offers began to flow in.

pops champagne

In total, I received offers from four different journals. Ultimately, I chose the *Indonesian Journal of International and Comparative Law*. (If you're interested in checking it out, it appears in Volume VII, Issue 4 (October 2020).)

After accepting the offer, the journal editor sent me a handful of comments and edits to consider before publication, and so

I tweaked a few points before resubmitting. He then requested a mailing address for my complimentary hard copies.

A few weeks later, I received a package from a sender I didn't recognize. *This does not look like an Amazon package... what could this be?* It contained two copies of the journal that my article appeared in: two dark blue, hardcover books featuring the journal title and a picture of some people on the front. I was euphoric because these hard copies represented the culmination of my blood, sweat, and tears. I flipped straight to page 541, and there it was—heading after heading and paragraph after paragraph of *my* published article. I could feel the pride well up inside me as I texted pictures of myself holding the journal to friends and family. I was sure to send a few photos to Professor Garrison's inbox, too. *Most importantly, I also posted the photo on Instagram. If something isn't posted on Instagram, did it even really happen?*

Getting this article published was important to me and vital to my success in multiple ways. First off, it was a great academic achievement. It's listed on my resume and often serves as a conversation-starter during interviews. But it also proved that I could take on a long-term challenge and see it all the way through. My bad experience at the real estate law firm damaged my confidence, and since then, nagging questions had kept me up at night: Could I be a good lawyer? Was I in the right field? Should I be doing something totally different? Did I waste my time? This article represented a much-needed win that boosted my confidence. *I wrote it from scratch and spent months outlining, researching, writing, editing, and rewriting... and now it was published.* I was a talented legal writer. I enjoyed reading legal articles, understanding complex legal topics, and hypothesizing about future legal developments. I was worthy of being a lawyer. I deserved to learn and grow, and I deserved mentors like Professor Garrison. Holding my published article was a fantastic ending to a publication journey that helped me to heal and believe in myself again.

Volunteering with the LGBT Bar Association

One day after work in March, I hopped on the 3 train and headed over to the LGBT Bar Association legal clinic. When I arrived,

I walked up the stairs and followed the line to a room that looked like a miniature classroom, with a few desks set up and chairs on either side. Some volunteers were sitting in front of open computers, getting ready to assist those who came to the clinic that night. There was a man standing in the doorway whose job was to ensure that everything was running smoothly and that the people waiting in the hall knew how much longer they would have to wait.

I was both nervous and excited to find out if I could volunteer. Even though I was happy in my new role at Société Genérale, there was still a part of me that questioned whether I was in the right field. I was not totally convinced that I was doing what I really wanted to do for the rest of my career. *What if I want to do something else? What if there is something that I'd like more than what I'm doing right now?* These thoughts would pop into my head sometimes as I was working or thinking about my career path.

As a law student, I participated in my law school's LGBT advocacy clinic. There, I worked on an adoption case for a same-sex couple, and I also worked on an immigration/asylum case for an individual claiming asylum in the United States because of harassment he received in his home country on account of his being gay. It was challenging but rewarding work. *Could I see myself continuing to work in LGBT family law or immigration law? Maybe?* I was not sure.

Volunteering with the LGBT Bar Association legal clinic was one way for me to try and figure this out. The legal clinic is set up to help people who have legal issues but who are not sure how to address them or who they should turn to for advice. It is staffed by volunteer lawyers who listen to their stories, identify potential legal issues, and provide them with low- or no-cost representation options.

I took a deep breath and walked up to the man in the doorway.

"Hi, I'm John Reilly. This is my first time here, but I was hoping to help by volunteering at the legal clinic."

"That's awesome. Nice to meet you, John. I'm Brett. Are you a lawyer?"

"Nice to meet you, too. I passed the bar and submitted my application, but I am waiting to officially be sworn into the New York Bar."

"Congratulations, that is exciting. Since you aren't admitted to the bar yet, you can't volunteer on your own. But if you'd like to shadow one of our lawyers here tonight, that may be a good way to get started."

"Sure thing, that sounds great to me."

Brett took me to one of the desks in the back of the room and introduced me to one of the volunteers, Ben. Ben showed me the forms that need to be filled out for each visitor and explained that each volunteer is usually assigned a handful of visitors each night. On this evening, three different visitors were assigned to Ben. One had a question about housing, the other about benefits, and the last about an immigration case. I watched as Ben kindly interacted with each person, helping to identify the relevant legal issues and eliciting their stories. After each encounter, Ben demonstrated how to complete the form and asked if I had any questions. Before I knew it, the evening was over. I thanked Ben and expressed my interest in volunteering with the clinic again.

When COVID-19 devastated New York just weeks later, the LGBT Bar Association legal clinic rapidly transformed from an in-person clinic to a virtual one. By April, I was admitted to the New York Bar and could then volunteer on my own, assisting clinic visitors virtually. This experience allowed me to work on skills that I was not necessarily using in my role at Société Genérale. At work, I was part of a corporate team focused on sanctions and business-related issues, whereas at the clinic, I worked individually with people seeking legal help and services. Some of them were dealing with criminal law issues, some with housing issues, some with immigration issues, and some with employment issues. Their concerns varied widely, and there was always something new for me to see.

Volunteering at the clinic necessarily meant dealing with different personalities. Some visitors were quiet or soft spoken, others loud and passionate. Some were very forthcoming and detailed about their concerns, while others needed to have the specifics drawn out of them through questioning. Working with so many people with different personalities helped to develop my active listening and communication skills, and it opened my eyes to how many people living in New York City urgently need legal aid. My empathy grew, and I was eager to provide good legal aid to my fellow New Yorkers.

Another benefit of working at the clinic was getting to know the director and other legal volunteers. Prior to the coronavirus, we would all chat in the waiting room before the clinic opened, or we would chat after the clinic closed, sometimes exchanging notes about the issues we encountered that day. But even after the coronavirus hit, forcing everyone to work from their homes, we continued to collaborate virtually. We still had conversations about who might be able to take on this case or that case. Our continued interactions during a time of isolation helped me to understand the paramount importance of community.

This volunteer experience was also personally enlightening and fulfilling. Even though it had been months since I left the real estate law firm, I was still shaken by my bad experience there, and my confidence was still shot. But volunteering helped me build up my confidence again. Whether it was someone's thanking me for listening to their story or helping them to find legal representation, or the clinic director's saying that I did a good job, the positive feedback I was getting was building up my confidence again. I started to think "Hey, I might be a good lawyer actually."

I volunteered with the clinic for about a year, and the experience played a fundamental role in my growth as a new lawyer. Through helping others, I was able to heal myself.

Teaching Pre-Bar Classes

While I was studying for the bar exam, I worked very closely with the academic success professors at Brooklyn Law School. As I was nearing the end of bar prep and getting ready to sit for the exam, my professor, Professor Flora Midwood, asked me a question that I wasn't ready for.

"I know I'm asking this in advance, but if things go according to plan and you pass the bar exam, would you want to come back for the next spring semester as a small group leader?"

Is this a good sign that she is asking me this? Does this mean she thinks I'll pass the exam the first time around? Oh God, what if I don't?

"Yeah, that would be great! I'm open to doing that."

Small group leaders (SGLs) are essentially alumni teacher's assistants (TAs) who help out with the pre-bar classes at Brooklyn Law School. About three times a semester, students submit their essay question responses to the SGLs who grade each answer, provide feedback, and review the essay question with the entire class. They also answer student questions about the bar exam, provide study tips, and sit on panels set up by the Academic Success Department to address student issues and concerns.

As a student, I worked closely with my SGL and always appreciated her feedback. I also enjoyed working with Professor Midwood and Professor Shane Dizon from the Academic Success Department. Assisting with the bar prep program was not something I had envisioned myself doing after law school, but the thought of getting to teach, work with students, and act as an advisor was exciting to me.

Months later, after passing the bar exam on my first attempt, I let Professor Midwood know that I was still interested in becoming an SGL.

At the beginning of the next semester, shortly after quitting my job at the real estate law firm, I participated in a calibration session with other SGLs and professors in the Academic Success Department. We read through a sample bar exam question and some sample answers, then discussed what grades we would assign each sample answer and why. This exercise helped all of us who would be grading students' answers to develop a standardized approach for doing so.

It was nice to be in a collaborative environment again. Everyone in the group was always respectful and had a genuine curiosity about others' different perspectives. Additionally, the work itself was interesting and rewarding. From a professional perspective, it enabled me to maintain my knowledge of the topics tested on the bar exam and further enhance my understanding of the bar exam. (*You may be asking why learning more about the bar exam after I had already passed it would be helpful to me. Keep reading!*) From a personal perspective, it was rewarding to work with students and mentor them. And, as someone who had a wonderful law school experience, it was a joy to return as an alumnus and stay involved in the community.

After the calibration session, I had a chance to catch up with Professor Midwood. I told her how (poorly) things had been going since I passed the bar and how happy I was to be helping out as an SGL. She said she was excited for me to be joining the Academic Success Department and that if I wanted to be an SGL for two sections instead of one, I could take on an extra class. I jumped at the chance.

Shortly after the calibration session, I received the syllabus, presentation materials, and essay questions that I would be reviewing with the students. I was free to build upon the existing presentation materials for the essay questions and to add a slide discussing additional bar prep strategies, such as picking a commercial bar prep company, setting a bar prep study schedule, and identifying the elective courses that are most helpful in preparing for the bar.

In anticipation of the first class meeting, I showed up at the law school extra early, printed all the materials I planned to hand out, reviewed/nearly memorized my presentation, and tried to anticipate all the questions that students might ask about this particular essay question.

Before I knew it, I was standing at the front of a classroom, facing about 15 students. The nerves inside me were fluttering like butterflies. But once I began speaking and interacting with the students, I forgot about the nerves. Everything went according to plan that day: I reviewed the essay and answered their follow-up questions about essay writing and the bar exam. And they were happy to hear that we'd end each class with a discussion of bar prep strategies.

After the students left, I took a deep breath. I did it. Class 1 is officially in the books. The three major feelings I had after that class were relief, pride, and hope.

I was relieved that I made it through the class without anything having gone wrong. *What if the presentation doesn't work? What if I don't know the answer to a student's question? What if the students hate me?* None of the what-ifs that I worried about came to fruition, and I had even kept my pre-class nervousness in check by relying on the work I put into preparing for the class and giving it all my best effort.

I was proud of the work I put into preparing the presentation, answering students' questions, and speaking publicly. This experience gave me insight into how much work teachers put into each and every lecture and class plan. *Shout out to every teacher whose class I've attended—thank you!* I believed that I was providing a valuable service by helping them to prepare for future careers in the legal field, and this belief motivated me.

I felt hopeful again about my future. Though I was still feeling crushed from my bad experience at the real estate firm, I was excited about being an SGL and thought that this experience could help me pick up the pieces and move forward. It gave me an opportunity to channel my energies into doing legal work that I was passionate about—helping students to prepare for the bar exam—and that would make a positive difference in students' lives. I no longer felt like my career in the legal profession was over.

Halfway into the spring semester, COVID-19 hit, and classes were canceled indefinitely. Nevertheless, I continued to meet with some students in one-on-one Zoom meetings to review their final practice essays. By the time summer bar prep came around, all courses had become 100 percent virtual, and I was tutoring some students one on one. Though virtual teaching was still unconventional at that time, I was happy to still be working with the Academic Success Department and helping students prepare for the bar exam, and I continued to teach virtual pre-bar classes during the 2020–2021 academic year.

Curveballs Are Not Always Negative

During the 2021 spring semester, a few professors I worked with let me know that a full-time position within the Academic Success Department would be opening up. The application and interview process would be rigorous and competitive, but I was extremely interested in the position. I figured that even if I didn't get hired for the position now, I could still show them how dedicated and qualified I am so that when the next full-time opportunity opened up, I would have a better chance of getting hired.

I immediately got to work on updating my resume and cover letter so that I could apply for the position as soon as it went up online. I knew this job opportunity was a long shot, but I knew I could succeed in the role if given the chance. A few weeks after I applied, I was invited in for an interview. I felt a mixture of excitement and determination. I was ready to prove to them that I was a good fit for the role, that I deserved to be a professor in the Academic Success Department.

One of the first things I did to prepare for my interview was to print out a copy of my resume and annotate it by hand. A resume is an effective tool for highlighting a potential candidate's responsibilities and achievements. *Duh.* But often, an interviewer wants to hear about different challenges and opportunities the interviewee has faced and how the interviewee handled them. I find annotating my resume to be a very helpful exercise because it forces me to sit down and rack my brain for different experiences worth sharing.

Prepare third-year law students for the bar exam by evaluating and grading MEE and MPT responses, providing feedback, developing in-class lessons, and answering questions.

Next to that sentence I added an annotation about the *In re Wendy Martel* MPT presentation (a bar exam essay question that is now used as a practice exam) I had put together. In a nutshell, my presentation focused on the importance of identifying the specific task at hand (in this case, writing an opinion letter) and how doing so helps to guide students' analysis. For a number of students, this was a breakthrough idea that led to improvements on their next practice MPT.

Provide one-on-one tutoring when students request extra help.

Here, I added an annotation about how one student stayed late after class to discuss tips for memorizing laws for the MEE portion of the exam. After that conversation, she was more open to asking questions and tutoring sessions, and she continued to reach out to me with questions during her commercial bar prep course. She passed the bar exam on the first try.

I utilized open-source Google searches and websites to help narrow down my search results to those questions that are asked frequently during interviews for professor roles or other roles in the academic success space. Knowing these FAQs gave me time to reflect on my experiences, think through my responses, and hone my messaging, which in turn boosted my confidence before the interview.

I also practiced my interview responses to these FAQs out loud. This helped me to get comfortable with speaking about my experiences and telling my story, which in turn made the interview itself seem less daunting. It also allowed me to work on and perfect my cadence and tone so that I could convey professionalism and confidence.

The interview question I spent the most time on was "Why should we hire you?"

Because I want this job really badly!

Because I'm beautiful just like you! Best looking department in the whole law school! #slay

Because if you don't hire me, I'll cry!

While I believe that all of those responses were valid, they probably weren't what the interviewer would be looking for. So I formulated an appropriate response to this question by reflecting on my education, experiences, and personality and stating why they made me the best fit for the job.

You should hire me because I have the education, experiences, and personality that make me the best fit for this position. As a former Brooklyn Law Student, I received an excellent legal education. I made sure to take bar prep classes to ensure my success on the exam. Not long after passing the bar exam on my first try, I returned to Brooklyn Law School to help mentor current students and prepare them to pass the bar exam on their first attempt as well. Working with the students and other professors in the Academic Success Department has been an extremely rewarding role for me. Working alongside dedicated colleagues and students who are eager to pass the bar exam and take the next step in their legal career brings me joy and motivates me to put in 110% of my effort into this role. I know that because of my dedication and eagerness to fill this position, I will fit in seamlessly with the Academic Success Department, and I am ready to take on this opportunity.

This particular interview process was broken into two stages. Stage one required a screening interview with the professors in the Academic Success Department. It was a relatively quick interview that gave me a chance to convey my genuine interest in the position. I wouldn't know whether I was being invited back for a second round of interviews until all screening interviews had been completed.

A few weeks, I received an email inviting me back for stage two. *Woohoo! This is going exactly according to plan!* It would be a full-day interview during which I would meet with multiple law school faculty members and administrators. *Conducted on Zoom of course! Thanks COVID-19!*

Oh my God, this is starting to become real. Could I actually get this position? Will I accept it? Yes, I would. Wait. We'll cross that bridge when I get there. Well, if I get there.

I was elated to be invited back for a second round of interviews. I quickly arranged an interview date and immediately resumed my interview prep.

When the big day came, I was in a full suit and tie, *including dress shoes.* Keep in mind that all of my interviews would be virtual and the screen would only show the top 20 percent of my body. But I was not taking any chances that day.

That day, I interviewed with professors outside the Academic Success Department, student ambassadors, administrators, faculty, and even the Vice President and President of the law school. *No pressure. No pressure at all.* I was asked some questions that I had prepared for and some that I had not. But thankfully I was able to answer questions in this latter category by weaving in various stories I had prepared in response to entirely different questions. I felt that my answers conveyed confidence and authenticity.

"What is your strategy for helping students who are not doing well in the class?"

What do you mean?! Every student I work with is amazing and will pass the bar exam on their first try!

This question was not one that I had anticipated and practiced. Nevertheless, I began to explain how students who struggle with the course often are not able to receive the testing accommodations that they need. I discussed how I'd work with students to ensure they have sufficient time to review materials and take practice exams, even if it meant letting them take practice exams outside of class, for example.

"Wow, that was actually one of the best answers to the question that I've heard. I'm impressed."

Whoa. Did I just impress the interviewer and he actually told me? I can't believe it!

I think that today kind of went well....

At the end of every interview, I made sure to request each interviewer's email address so that I could send them a personalized thank you email, which I did the next day. Then I waited and checked my email. Then I waited and checked my email again. And on and on. As days turned into weeks, I started to realize that I probably was not going to get the job. But I still felt really proud of the hard work I put into preparing for the interviews and how well I performed during them. Regardless of the outcome, the whole experience was another step toward rebuilding my confidence.

As summer approached, I received an unexpected phone call from Professor Dizon.

"Hey, we filled the full-time professor role with another candidate, but would you be interested in becoming an adjunct for the Academic Success Department? You could teach two classes a semester and expand into the Academic Success courses for 1Ls and 2Ls."

It was not the result I had expected, but I was thrilled nonetheless and accepted the offer. He then gave me various resources to use in preparing for the upcoming fall semester.

So much for thinking I would have to choose between my current job at Société Genérale and a new job at Brooklyn Law. Now I'm going to have two jobs!

I was particularly excited because the classes I was teaching would be in-person classes. No more little boxes with people's faces in them. These would be interactive, face-to-face classes. *A novel idea, I know.*

Early on in the fall semester, I realized that being an adjunct professor was a much bigger responsibility than being an SGL. I spent the days before class pouring over the syllabus, preparing notes and presentations, and making sure the online class portal was up to date. I learned many valuable lessons as an adjunct, including (1) teaching is a time-consuming profession, and balancing two jobs at once is a lot; (2) teaching requires a lot of patience; and (3) watching one of your students recognize their own improvement thanks to your help is the best feeling ever.

A few days before I started teaching, I was able to catch up with my mentor and former professor, Professor Garrison. I chatted about how my summer went and how excited I was to be teaching in the upcoming semester.

"I'm going to be teaching Pre-Bar I and Pre-Bar II this semester and then Pre-Bar II and Legal Analysis Seminar for 1Ls next semester."

"Two classes each semester! That is going to be a lot of work! Be prepared to spend some time preparing for class, answering emails, and grading exams."

In hindsight, I see that she was gently warning me about how busy the next few months would be for me. But I was bright eyed and bushy-tailed, so I just thought she was just wishing me good luck.

I was fortunate because syllabi, selected texts for review and homework, and presentations already existed for my classes. Working off of these would make it easier to prepare for my lectures. But, even with these preexisting materials, it still took me a lot of time to prepare. That's because I still had to read and review the assignments myself, mark them up, take notes, and anticipate student questions. In a way it was like doing homework all over again, even though I was the professor. *It's just that this time, I will be the one cold-called on in every class and responsible for answering all the questions. No pressure!*

In my PowerPoint presentations, I would include not only pre-bar materials but also class reminders/notices, school-wide announcements, and upcoming programs sponsored by the Academic Success Department. Depending on the class, my presentations might involve looking at multiple-choice practice questions and strategizing how to approach them, or reviewing a practice essay question to identify different ways to answer it correctly and various pitfalls to avoid. For example, when it comes to multiple-choice, the answer is black and white: three options are wrong, only one is right. But with essays, there are multiple ways to craft a successful answer, *as well as multiple traps*. This set the stage for all different types of student questions:

"If I included the right elements of the law but not the facts, will I still get points?"

"Wait, I did the opposite. I forgot some of the elements of the law but mentioned all the facts. What about my response?

"I truly had no idea where to even start this response so I didn't even get to the law or fact application sections."

Not once during my entire academic career did I stop and consider how much my professors had to prepare prior to class to be ready to answer any question thrown at them. *I don't even remember any teachers breaking a sweat trying to answer any questions!* Yet here I was, sweating it out, hoping that I would not look like a fraud or a failure for not being able to answer something.

Fortunately, my class preparation routine was effective—but it was *really* time consuming. Working a full-time day job at Société Genérale and teaching at night meant that I didn't have as much free time on my hands as I used to. I spent my weekends and "off" nights preparing for my lectures. Making things even more difficult was that one of my pre-bar classes didn't have a small group leader assigned to it, which meant I was also responsible for teaching some of the small group lessons and reviews.

How did I go from having no legal jobs to having two?! Is this a good thing? Am I overcompensating for that one bad job? Oh well!

In order to keep up with my workload, I needed to make some sacrifices, like skipping lawyer networking events, turning down happy hours and other social events, and canceling some weekend plans. I liked my full-time job at Société Genérale and needed it to pay my bills, and I also really liked teaching at Brooklyn Law and staying connected to the law school community. But doing both at the same time was a lot of work and advanced planning.

As an SGL who helped out with two classes, I only had to spend a couple of days every month preparing for class. But as an adjunct professor teaching two semester-long classes, almost every day involved some kind of class prep. This increased responsibility was both exciting and stressful. *Depending on the day, it could feel like a lot more of one than the other.* But, even though it was a lot of work, I knew that I was fortunate to be teaching law school classes at such an young age and so early on in my legal career. Putting things into perspective and keeping a mindset of gratitude kept me inspired and gave me the motivation to continue doing my best.

You went from being unemployed and wondering if you would ever make it in the legal field, to literally teaching at law school and working a full-time job. Keep your head up! Keep going!

I am New York City born and raised. I walk fast. I talk fast. I do not like to wait. I like to get things done quickly and then move on to the next thing. Patience is not my strongest quality. But taking on this teaching role not only forced me to figure out how to balance a busy work schedule but also taught me how to be patient. When I was first hired as an adjunct, I visualized myself in a classroom, engaging students in interesting conversations, helping them to improve their legal writing skills, and watching students grasp a better understanding of the law. I did not imagine battles with the online portal, technical issues preventing my in-class presentation materials from loading, or juggling multiple email chains with students or other faculty members. Yet I did all of those things. Daily.

At Société Genérale, although I worked on a team, each of us was expected to be more or less self-sufficient, relying mostly on ourselves to get our jobs done. Although we could ask each other questions or discuss new issues, for the most part we were expected to take the lead on our own projects and see them through.

But teaching requires much more teamwork and team effort. *Much more than I expected.* There were moments when I was truly stuck and had to rely on others—whether students, faculty, or IT—to help me solve a problem. But most of the time, others were asking things of me: as a professor, I'd receive numerous questions from both students and faculty. On any given day, I might hear from a student asking whether they could make up the work from a class they missed, a student asking about my grading system and whether it was still possible for them to get an A in the course, or an academic success professor following up on a student's progress. I needed to manage a variety of relationships: sometimes, I needed to manage up to the other professors and deans, and other times, I needed to manage down to students and address their questions and concerns.

Often, these dialogues could play out across days or sometimes weeks. As someone who strongly prefers quick resolutions, I needed to learn patience. I came to understand that people's priorities and to-do lists can vary, and so keeping an open line of communication may be necessary to get things done. For me, that meant keeping a running list of ongoing projects and becoming proactive about following up with others when certain issues remained unresolved for too long. This helped to prevent issues from falling by the wayside, only to resurface in the form of an urgent request or call down the line, at a most inconvenient time (e.g., right before a final or when grades are due).

Managing these different relationships was an exercise in not only patience but grace. Back when I was just a student, I wouldn't think about it too much when certain students would miss a lot of classes or ask a lot of questions. But being a professor made me more aware of different outside circumstances that students might be dealing with that could impact their academic performance. Some had health complications or families with health complications. Others worked full-time day jobs and had families to take care of. For any number of reasons, I might have to offer extra guidance or one-on-one instruction to help students succeed in the classroom. I hadn't necessarily expected any of this when I began teaching, but understanding the importance of my role in students' success was fulfilling, and it motivated me to give my all and show up for them. And yet, though I always gave my best, *sometimes I fell short.*

As the next second semester rolled around, I went through much the same motions as the last time: review the syllabi, start reading the class materials, put the presentations together. I also compiled a worksheet listing the daily class homework assignments that were due for each class.

At the beginning of my third Pre-Bar II class of the semester, as I getting myself organized, I saw a student raise his hand to ask a question.

"Hey, how can I help you today?" I asked cheerily.

"I have a quick question about the Essay 1 homework: was it due today or next week? The syllabus says it's due today, but the homework assignment worksheet says it is due next week."

I quickly scramble the papers in front of me so that I can cross-reference the syllabus and the homework assignment worksheet.

Ah, shit.

"You're right, it looks like I mixed up the date on the homework assignment worksheet. No worries though, just bring it to class next week, and you'll receive full credit."

"Just bring it to class next week? Are you f***ing kidding me? How is it acceptable that the dates are wrong on a sheet that *you* gave out?"

Did I just hear that right? Did he curse at me?

I was at a loss for words. Was this student really mad about a homework assignment that I said he could still submit for credit?

"Listen, it's not a big deal. Just submit it next week, and you'll receive credit."

The student became visibly agitated and started screaming from the back of the classroom.

"You gotta be f***ing kidding me. This is unacceptable. How is this acceptable at all that you're giving homework assignments and don't have the same dates on both papers. I was looking at the wrong sheet, and now I don't have the homework for today."

Is he still cursing at me? And screaming at me? What the hell is wrong with him? Can I scream back at him? Is that unprofessional?

"Listen, it was a typo and it happens. We're all living through the COVID-19 pandemic. It's not the biggest deal in the world."

"COVID?!" He screamed, "you're trying to blame this on COVID?"

Okay, this conversation is going on for too long. Abort mission. Abort mission.

"Listen, I'm giving you the option to hand in the homework next week. Do it or don't. But you are being extremely unprofessional and that's unacceptable. I've never heard anyone speak to a professor like this. This conversation is over."

"Are you kidd—"

"This conversation is over!"

You could hear a pin drop. I don't think I've ever had all eyes on me in a classroom like that before, and I don't think I will again. My heart was racing a million miles a minute as I continued to get organized before the lecture. *How am I supposed to teach for two hours now? What's this class even about?* I only had a few more minutes before class began, at which point the awkwardness faded away quickly as we moved through the material. But that exchange remained in the forefront of my mind for the next few weeks.

Could I have done something differently? Should I have done something differently? Should I have kicked him out of class? Should I have just kicked him?

Yes, I made an error on the homework assignment sheet that led to this students' not submitting his homework on the day it was due. But his reaction in this situation was clearly out of line and not one that I was prepared for. He had screamed at me more aggressively than any of the lawyers at the real estate firm. *Should I really be using that law firm as a bar for how to treat people? No. But it is still relevant here.*

I played out multiple scenarios in my head to try and justify his overreaction. Maybe he was having a rough day. Maybe he had just received really bad news at work and was not mentally prepared to sit through class. Maybe this was just on brand for this student. There are truly any number of possible explanations for his behavior.

Whatever the reason, I still had to continue teaching him for the rest of the semester. Even though it was a jarring experience, I still learned a few valuable lessons: (1) each of us has to live with our own actions; (2) you will not get along with everyone and may even get disrespected by some people, but you still need to work together;

and (3) the best thing you can do is not allow bad interactions to consume you—you must learn to let go.

Each of us has to live with our own actions. I couldn't help but question how this student could show up to class and look me in the eye for the rest of the semester. Sometimes I still wonder what would have happened if I made a formal complaint to the law school about his behavior. But, at the end of the day, I'm proud of how I responded to the situation. I kept my cool, offered a fair solution (he could have just submitted the homework for credit the following week), and ended the conversation before it got completely out of hand. I was hired to teach law students, and I take that responsibility extremely seriously. Professionalism is also important to me. "You cannot control anyone else, but you can control yourself and your actions" is advice that I apply to all aspects of my life, and I believe that it served me well in this situation.

You will not get along with everyone and may even get disrespected by some people, but you still need to work together. When I left the real estate law firm I was concerned that I did not have thick enough skin for the legal profession. *What if I want to avoid confrontation as much as possible? How can I even be a lawyer?* But this experience taught me that I can work with people I don't necessarily get along with or who are rude to me, and I was proud of myself. It is a fact of life that you will not get along with every person you meet. Maybe some just rub you the wrong way. Maybe others scream at you for making an error on the syllabus. Here, I reacted to a completely inappropriate overreaction in a professional manner and did not run away. The student continued to show up for class, and I continued to perform my job well and even answer his questions. Dealing with unpleasant or downright unlikeable people without allowing their negativity to affect you is a really important skill that can be developed.

The best thing you can do is not allow bad interactions to consume you—you must learn to let go. This interaction with the student consumed me for weeks. I would dwell on it when I was alone, talk about it with my partner and family, and think about it during my day job at Société Genérale. I was consumed by embarrassment and kept wondering whether I should have reacted differently.

But, as already noted, over time I decided that I was proud of how I conducted myself, and I realized that the problem was not me but rather the student. Once I had come to terms with what had happened, I let go of the stress, anxiety, and embarrassment I had been dragging me down. I then moved forward, carrying only the valuable lessons I had learned from the experience.

This difficult experience was definitely not the norm for me at the law school. As an adjunct professor, I worked closely with the students and small group leaders in my classes and built relationships with them. It was the most satisfying aspect of my job. Introducing students to the bar exam can be nerve wracking: the amount of information that students are tested on over the course of two days is massive, and covering everything in class that needs to be covered can feel overwhelming. But my students appreciated my efforts and my ability to break things down into more manageable pieces, and they were genuinely interested in hearing about my personal experiences regarding the bar exam and studying for law school exams.

For example, in one class, I displayed two versions of the same exam answer on the big screen. On the left-hand side, the answer was in one giant paragraph. On the right-hand side was the answer broken down into multiple paragraphs, separated into issue, rule, application, and conclusion sections. This visual demonstrated how much easier it is for teachers and exam graders to process information when it's broken down into multiple paragraphs. After class, a student came up to me and thanked me for giving that visual explanation. She said that she had not been breaking up her exam answers into multiple paragraphs and was excited to use this new technique moving forward. Seeing a student so excited after one of my classes (*especially a night class!*) really warmed my heart. I was happy that the time and effort that I put into this lesson really paid off big time for one of my students. Her excitement and engagement motivated and inspired me to keep putting in 110 percent effort.

Teaching also forced me to learn how to manage my time more efficiently. This skill became especially relevant in fall 2021—when the start of my third semester of teaching coincided with the start a new full-time job. *Spoiler alert! See more in the next chapter!* I knew that things were about to get very busy and chaotic and that, to stay on top of everything, I'd have to be extremely intentional with my time. For me, this meant blocking off large chunks of time specifically for classroom prep. I would spend hours every weeknight and entire weekends preparing for my classes so that I could continue to give my students my best. I eventually became exhausted from trying to keep up with the demands of juggling two roles. So, while teaching and interacting with students was still rewarding for me, I eventually made the difficult decision to stop teaching for the time being to focus on my new job. However, I told myself that if an opportunity presented itself down the line and the timing was right, I would head right back into the classroom again.

9

Is It Already Time for a New Job? Looking for Your Next Legal Role

"So you may have seen this coming," Eric says over the phone. I feel the nerves start to kick in. My heart starts to race.

"You got a new job?" I half ask, half confirming what I already know.

"I got a new job," he says. "Just got an offer I couldn't turn down. I'll be here for another month to answer any questions you have and pass off any responsibilities that you might want to take from me to build up your resume."

"Thank you," I say. "I really appreciate that."

Eric was the ideal colleague for someone at their first (or second?) professional job: He was whip smart. He was accessible and could transfer his knowledge to the team with ease. He was always kind. Losing him was a tough blow to the team, but it was not totally unexpected. Over the past few months, multiple mid-level managers had left to pursue different opportunities that they just could not turn down either, so it seemed only a matter of time before the same thing would start to happen at the associate level.

At the time Eric gave his notice, I had been at Société Genérale for just over two years. After he told me, I seriously began, for the second time, to consider looking for a new job and was curious to see what else was out there.

The second time? When was the first time? Great question! It was a few months into my job at Société Genérale. Even as I was learning about the sanctions field and getting into the swing of things, I still had lingering doubts about whether I was in the right role. Maybe I wanted to switch practice areas and work as a family lawyer at an LGBTQ+ focused law firm. And so I'd peruse LinkedIn and search on Google for associate attorney positions with these types of law firms, usually without much luck. Then, one day, I found a job posting for an associate attorney position at a LGBTQ+ focused law firm in New Jersey. Being from Brooklyn, the location was not ideal for me, but the job description was. I applied immediately and waited anxiously for a response. Surprisingly, just a few days later, I received an email from the firm asking to set up an interview.

The interview went well. I talked about how excited I was to start working for a firm that helps LGBTQ+ people. They joked about saving a Brooklyn gay from the compliance world. We laughed. Within a week I was offered the job.

Quite suddenly, my excitement turned to panic. Was I going to leave my job at Société Genérale, a job that I only had for a few months, to become an LGBTQ+ family lawyer? At that moment, I truly didn't know. So I spoke with my partner and with my parents.

What am I going to do? Taking a leap and accepting this new LGBTQ+ family lawyer job could be really interesting. But I've just started to get in the swing of things in the sanctions field. Maybe I'll be able to help more people as an LGBTQ+ family lawyer? But I won't be getting paid well, and I'll sometimes have to commute to New Jersey from Brooklyn, which is not ideal. These are two very different career paths... Why is it so hard for me to decide which path I want to take? Why do I put myself in these positions?

I talked myself in circles. I was still wounded from my bad experience at the real estate law firm. I still felt twinges of regret over accepting that job. While most of that regret stemmed from having to work with colleagues who were difficult or had challenging personalities, part of it had to do with the fact that I had no interest in real estate law. For both of these reasons, I was now pressuring myself to find the perfect job—one where I enjoyed being around my colleagues and was passionate about the work.

I had respond to the LGBTQ+ family law firm by Monday. That Sunday evening, I sat with my partner and called my parents and told them that I was planning to accept their job offer. Even though the pay was less than I was currently making, and even though I would sometimes have to go to New Jersey, I had decided that it was the right fit for me. They all congratulated me and were supportive of my move.

The next morning, I sat down at my laptop, fully intending to accept the job offer. Instead, I found that I could not bring myself to type the words "I accept your offer." *Wait, what is going on here? You were so confident yesterday!* At the time, I couldn't put my feelings into words. I just knew that I was experiencing a change of heart. Looking back, I realize I was experiencing "motion sickness" from jumping so quickly from my first job out of law school to my second job. Jumping to yet another job in such a short span of time would only worsen the motion sickness that I was already experiencing. On top of that, I wasn't sure that I wanted to leave the sanctions field. I was still very new at Société Genérale and learning a lot—I didn't know enough about the sanctions field to make an informed decision about whether it was right for me.

I ultimately turned down the job offer. Later that evening, I explained my decision to my partner and my parents. Everyone was understandably surprised given the conversation we had a day earlier. To be candid, I think they all had a little bit of motion sickness from my career journey, too. But they were supportive and reminded me that my happiness was paramount.

Flash forward about a year and a half so that we are back where this chapter started—Eric has announced his resignation and I'm thinking about searching for a new job again. But this time feels different. My job search following my resignation from the real estate law firm was conducted in a state of panic. So was the job search that led me to the LGBTQ family law firm. I was panicked during those job searches because I was a recent law school grad without any substantial full-time employment experience. My negative experience at the real estate firm had shaken me to the core, and I also felt a general sense of unease about my career. But, after two years at Société Genérale, I had some sanctions expertise, full-time legal experience, and confidence. This time, I would not be scrambling to find any employer in the legal field who would hire me. I would not scour Google and LinkedIn and submit my resume for any role I might be qualified for. I was becoming a confident lawyer, and I would tailor my job search accordingly.

As I contemplated my next career move, I developed a plan. I would (1) think about why I wanted to switch jobs; (2) outline what I needed in my next job, what I wanted in my next job, and what my non-negotiables were; (3) talk to my network about potential new jobs and job opportunities; (4) apply for new jobs; and (5) prepare for the interview.

Step 1: What Is Your Why?

The first step in this process is to determine your "why." *Why do I want to switch jobs?* For me there were a few reasons/precipitating events. First, some middle-management level colleagues had begun to leave Société Genérale for jobs with higher salaries and better job titles. As they left, their work was distributed among those who remained at the company. Although some new folks were hired to replace them, most of their work was assigned to associates, like myself. On the one hand, this was a great opportunity for us associates to do more interesting work and get a better sense of how the sanctions compliance team was run. On the other hand, this led to our working longer hours without a salary or title increase to reflect the extra work we were doing. Meanwhile, most of us associate-level employees were expecting that the most senior associate would be promoted to a middle-management position, given the company history of promoting the most senior associate every two to three years. When this did not happen, those of us at the associate level felt surprised and demoralized. We got the feeling that opportunities for growth within Société Genérale were limited and that perhaps there were opportunities elsewhere offering more growth potential.

On top of this, I personally felt that I had grown a lot in my current position and that I could excel in another role with more responsibilities (*and better pay!*). As I talked about above, I had two years of experience at Société Genérale under my belt. I had learned a lot about the sanctions field and was becoming a subject matter expert. I knew that I had transferable skills and that I could build upon my existing knowledge base in a new role. I wanted new responsibilities that would allow me to grow and learn even more about the field.

Moving up in law school and moving up in your legal career are very different experiences. Everything in school is organized so neatly. You know exactly how many classes you need to take and how many credits you need to earn to graduate. You get syllabi and final schedules to let you know how much time you have to study for a test or hand in a paper. Once you check all the boxes, you get a diploma to prove it. When it comes to your legal career, however, there are no syllabi or final schedules, no end dates or winter breaks. No one tells you if you've been at a job for too long or haven't been there long enough. No professor tells you whether you've learned enough in your current role or whether you still have more to learn. You must evaluate your own situation to determine whether it's time to search for a new job. That means determining your potential for growth within your current company. It means assessing your skillset and benchmarking the progress you're making.

Step 2: What Do You Want or Need from Your Next Job?

Once you've decided that you're ready to start looking for another job, you should create a list of things that you want to do in your next position and a list of things that you do not want to do. A good starting point for this exercise is to look at your current responsibilities. But you should also consider whether there are things you might like to do but haven't had the opportunity yet.

As a sanctions compliance associate, I grew to love the sanctions field, especially from a policy perspective. Staying abreast of sanctions trends and updates to regulations was interesting to me. I enjoyed sharing that information within my own team and with other business lines, and I also enjoyed offering other teams advice on sanctions issues. So I knew that I wanted my next role to be in sanctions.

Over time, I really came to enjoy compiling the team metrics. I viewed this responsibility as an asset for a couple of reasons. One, because most of my colleagues didn't want to deal with numbers and found them confusing—they appreciated that I did this work so that they didn't have to. Two, I enjoyed that I could see internal team trends and use that information to communicate with management, explaining how resources were being used and predicting what we would need in the future. It would be a definite plus to find a new position that included handling such metrics.

But there were aspects of my role that I didn't enjoy as much or felt that I had outgrown, for example, analyzing individual transactions to determine whether a true sanctions nexus existed. When I was still new, this part of the role was interesting and a helpful way for me to learn about different sanctions programs and how they are implemented in real time. However, this task was extremely time-consuming and, and after two years of doing this analysis, I was just seeing the same issues repeatedly. I felt it was an aspect of the job that I had outgrown. So I knew that, moving forward, I wanted a role where I would provide more guidance and counsel from a policy perspective and be less involved at a transactional level. Add this to my "do not want" list.

Something I knew I needed was a hybrid or fully remote work schedule. At the time I was job hunting in 2022, I was working from home three days a week and in the office two days a week, but there were rumors that soon we would be required to come into the office three days a week. I had grown accustomed to the hybrid work schedule and really liked the flexibility of being able to choose which days I would work remotely and which days I'd work in the office. I knew that I did not want a job that required me to be in the office more than two days a week.

I also needed any new job to come with a salary bump and more senior job title. With two years of experience, I was no longer considered entry level and could therefore pursue higher paying opportunities. I was excited to use my experience as leverage in seeking a better position with better pay.

Although it is probably obvious at this point, by the time I had decided to leave Société Genérale, I knew that I wanted to focus on growing my career in the sanctions field. Though I had previously considered working in LGBTQ+ family law or as a full-time professor, I had come to realize that sanctions was the best fit for me. I knew that if I wanted to pursue future opportunities in LGBTQ+ law or in teaching that I would be able to leverage my prior experience in those areas. But for right now, I just wanted to grow in the area I was in.

With that said, I wanted to explore careers outside of the banking industry. I knew that a lot of private companies, and financial technology companies in particular, had a need for sanctions counsel, and the prospect of expanding my knowledge into one of those industries excited me. Working in a different industry could be a great way for me to build upon my existing knowledge base.

Step 3: Tell Your Network That You Are Looking for New Opportunities

After you've identified your wants and needs, the next step is to let those in your network know that you are searching for a new job.

One of the most important conversations I had when I began to think about leaving Société Genérale was with my mentor, Russ. He was a neutral third party who could give me general advice about switching jobs and what to look out for, but he could also offer me more specific and nuanced advice regarding the legal field. He assured me that my timing was also typical—he said that entry-level employees tended to start looking for new jobs after about two years.

Russ also offered to connect me with some of his contacts who are also lawyers in the sanctions/regulatory field. Each of them was willing to get on the phone with me and share their advice about breaking into the field and finding new opportunities there. They gave advice based on their personal experiences, and each offered different types of help. One contact said he was happy to review my resume and provide me with suggestions on how to better explain my professional experience and how that experience transfers over into another legal role. Another contact I spoke with put me in touch with another colleague of his. Yet another contact knew of a job at his firm that matched some but not all of my interests, and he told me to reach out to him if I decided that I wanted to apply for it. All of these conversations were opportunities for me to more succinctly explain why I was seeking a new job and to tweak my elevator pitch. I was constantly taking in new information and using it to help myself evaluate what I wanted in my next job.

Another way to build and expand your network is through recruiters. You can search LinkedIn for legal recruiters or reach out to your network for recommendations. Recruiters have insight into which companies are hiring and what qualities they're looking for in potential candidates. They often are aware of/are actively trying to hire someone for roles that are not posted online or otherwise publicly available. And because recruiters are eager to find lawyers to fill open jobs, they can be a very helpful and motivated resource.

I spoke with a recruiter who Eric had put me in touch with. Unfortunately, the recruiter had more positions in the compliance space than in the legal space, so our conversation did not directly lead to an interview or job offer. But, on the plus side, the recruiter had become yet another contact in my network: we agreed to keep in touch and keep the door open for future job opportunities.

Step 4: Apply

If it's been a while since you've searched for a job, it's likely you've forgotten that applying for a job is a multi-step process.

LinkedIn has always been my starting point. I like that it has a user-friendly format, many employers post jobs there, and it's a great way to find out more about a company and team.

Before applying to a job on LinkedIn, I would always read its description and try to (1) gauge my general level of interest in the job and (2) see if there were any unexpected pros or cons, or one of my non-negotiables, listed among the job requirements. Reading through numerous job descriptions can help you to build an internal data set of rules and responsibilities that interest or inspire you, as well as those that do not interest you or do not align with your non-negotiables. But to better gauge your general interest level in a particular job, look beyond the surface level (i.e., role and responsibilities) and try to learn more about other important factors, including company culture, the physical working environment, and benefits.

A helpful threshold question to ask yourself during this process is "Do I think I would be happy doing this job for a week? Three months? Six months? A year? Two years?" This will force you to think about a role in both the short and long term. It will force you to parse through the roles and responsibilities from the perspective of whether you can see yourself learning and growing in the role in the long term. *Of course, you will also encounter job descriptions that make you say "never not even for one second in my lifetime would I even think about applying for this job." Hopefully, however, the LinkedIn algorithm will filter out most of these jobs based on your searches so that you don't have to waste your time on them.*

Keep a running list of all the jobs that interest you. This will allow you to compare them to each other and make it easier to choose which ones you ultimately want to apply to. As you do so, make sure to scour each job description for any non-negotiables that make the job a bad fit for you. Because a non-negotiable is, by definition, something that you must or must not have, viewing each job on your list through the lens of your non-negotiables is one of the more clear-cut ways to assess whether a job is right for you.

As I began to search for my third post-law school job, I reflected on my experience at Société Genérale to help form my non-negotiables. For example, I knew that I enjoyed the sanctions field and that there were options to move forward in both the compliance space and the legal space. However, after working in the compliance space for a couple of years, I knew that I wanted to find a role where I could use my knowledge to address sanctions issues from a legal rather than a compliance perspective.

As I mentioned earlier, I needed my next role to be a hybrid or fully remote one. Identifying this as a non-negotiable helped me to narrow down which jobs I would or would not apply for. Some employers required four or five days in the office, some required one or two, and some required none. *Some companies don't even have offices—what a smart real estate decision!* Because I had decided in advance that I would pursue only roles that were fully remote or required a maximum of two days per week in the office, I was able to easily eliminate some jobs from consideration. It helped me to fight the instinct to apply to every possible position and see what sticks.

Applying for your second (or third?) job out of law school can be quite different from your initial post-law school job search. It is not uncommon for more recent graduates to have a "beggars can't be choosers" mentality. But when you are currently employed have years of experience under your belt, you can be more selective. You don't need to apply for or accept positions you are ambiguous about. You have the freedom to focus on finding the perfect fit.

While non-negotiables can help you weed out the non-starters, discovering unexpected pros can help to raise a particular job in your rankings. Perhaps these pros are inherent in the role itself. For example, as I was searching on LinkedIn, I prioritized sanctions roles that involved working closely with compliance teams. I believed that I could really leverage the experience I gained at Societe Generale in such roles. Alternatively, the pros might relate to company culture or benefits. For example, some organizations offer "summer Fridays," i.e., half days on Fridays during the summer months. Some offer extremely generous PTO and 401K plans. Such perks are important to consider in addition to the job itself.

Of course, you don't need to/shouldn't limit your job search to what's on LinkedIn. A Google search is a great way to find job postings that may not appear on LinkedIn. Additionally, and also obviously, Google is great for looking up company websites, where you can explore and maybe get a feel for the company's company culture or benefits. You can also use it to see how well a company is doing financially and whether they are in the news. Depending on what you find online, you may be more or less inclined to apply for a job with that company than you were when you started.

After you're satisfied with the number of jobs you have on your running list, it's time to divide them into different categories.

Based on your wants and needs, determine which jobs you will definitely apply to now. Place the remaining jobs on a "reserve and revisit" list that you can return to depending on how your job search goes. Doing this will not only help you to finalize your plan of attack but also help you to keep the application process neat and organized.

Now it's time to begin the actual process of applying to your top jobs. In some cases, that might entail not much more than updating a few dates and minor details on your resume prior to submitting it. But putting in a little extra time and effort to truly tailor your resume to each specific role could increase the chances of being offered an interview.

You could start by updating/tweaking the most recent resume you sent out. But you could also take a different approach that involves using something called a "master resume." A master resume contains all of your work and academic experience, i.e., it is comprehensive and not tailed to any particular job. Lawyers in the early stage of their careers are advised to have a resume that is no more than one page long, but a master resume can be any length. Depending on what you are applying to, you will pull different information from your master resume to create a shorter resume that is tailored to the role. For example, my master resume included my experience at Societe Generale, my teaching experience, my volunteer work, and my educational experiences. Depending on what I was applying to, I would, for example, include my volunteer work and exclude my teaching experience. Having all of my relevant experience in one centralized master resume made it much easier for me to create bespoke resumes for particular roles.

After you've decided which experience to include on your resume, next step is to connect your experiences to what is laid out in the job description. To do this, use language identical to that in the job description and add examples to support your claim that you have this skill. (*Hey, that is what the artificial intelligence filters like to see!*) For example, if a job description states that the candidate will have to meet tight deadlines, you need to show in your resume that you have that experience. In my case, I explained that I was responsible for my team's monthly metrics and that I consistently delivered them on time to senior management. Similarly, if a job description states that a candidate must have prior experience in successfully dealing with multiple internal stakeholders, you need to show in your resume that you have that experience. I demonstrated prior success in navigating and managing multiple internal stakeholders by describing how I provided updates on sanctions regulations and explained the impacts of these updates to the various business lines that were affected.

Making sure that the language in your resume mirrors the job description is especially important nowadays because many companies use software that filters out job applications based on keywords. The more keywords you use, the more likely it is that your resume will be seen, and the fewer keywords you use, the less likely it is that your resume will be seen. *So, should you just copy and paste the job description into your resume and see what happens? Well, I haven't tried it, so I can't definitively say that it won't work. Give it a shot, and let me know how it goes!*

As you create each new resume, save each one to a resume folder on your computer using the following naming convention: "Resume - Company Name That You Applied To". This will help you to easily keep track of your resumes. If there is one thing that the job application process makes clear, it is that a resume is not a static document. It is a snapshot of your experiences up to a certain point in time. As such, it requires periodic updating and tweaking.

Sometimes applying to a job requires more than just submitting a resume. A job posting may require submitting a cover letter, answering a questionnaire, or filling out an application form. Each of these additional requirements serves an important function. For instance, cover letters can serve to weed out less serious applicants because they can be time-consuming and many people simply hate writing them. *Oh my God, this is my dream job. I can't wait to apply... Oh, wait. I need to submit a cover letter? Never mind. I would literally rather do anything else.*

Despite being time-consuming, writing a good cover letter has its benefits. As mentioned above, a cover letter requirement might help you to assess your true level of interest in a particular job. If you simply cannot bring yourself to write one, you're probably not as interested in the job as you think you are. But, assuming that you are interested enough to put one together, a cover letter can be an early opportunity to sell yourself and demonstrate why you are the right fit for the role. Writing your cover letter is similar to building your resume—the idea is to connect your experiences to what the employer is looking for in a candidate—but with the caveat that you should not restate in your cover letter what is already said in your resume. *Are you sure? Can't I just use my new updated resume that already uses the keywords?! The filter will love that!*

Using the resume example from five paragraphs up, if your resume already highlights how you are effective at meeting tight deadlines and dealing with multiple stakeholders, then your cover letter should highlight other skills that appear in the job description. Perhaps your cover letter could highlight your communication skills, your ability to work well with others, or your knowledge of and ability to keep up with industry trends. You could also use your cover letter to highlight interests you have that aren't directly connected to the job description but are still relevant. For example, if a company does volunteer work with another organization that you are passionate about or something about the company's mission statement really speaks to you, it might be a good idea to say so in your cover letter. The cover letter is your opportunity to articulate why you are interested in a job and why you are a good fit in your own words. *I'm interested in this job because I love the volunteer work your company does, and also... I need more money.* In a nutshell, having a solid cover letter in addition to a solid resume can help you to build a stronger case for yourself, giving you greater odds of reaching the interview stage.

Some jobs require candidates to fill out application forms that contain questions relating to a specific role or specific qualifications. Such questions are designed so that a filter can rank individual applications. In my experience, these application forms usually require little more than copying and pasting from my resume and checking yes or no for certain job qualifications (e.g., Can you legally work in the United States? Do you have at least two years of work experience after law school?) *Has work ever made you cry next to Elmo in Times Square? Ya know, just the basic questions here.*

As with cover letters, these application forms may serve to weed out less interested or less qualified candidates.

A Fun Tangent Based on Job Requirements

It can be disheartening when you are forced to select an option on an application form that seems to disqualify you from a job. For example, one time an application form asked whether I had three years of experience after law school, and I had to select "no" because I only had two years of post-law school professional experience. I knew that selecting "no" likely meant that my resume would not be seen by the employer. *Oh, come on, I'm so great otherwise! Just look at my resume. I have all the other skills you required on your job posting!*

While you may not meet every requirement listed in a job description, it is nevertheless important to apply to jobs that you are genuinely interested in and can see yourself succeeding in.

So, can I go from being an associate to applying for CEO jobs? I'm ready! I can do it! I'm confident, and I used the keywords from the job description to fill out my application! Put me at the top of the list!

Well, not quite. You must use your best judgment to determine whether you are qualified for a particular role, or whether it is worth your time to apply for a job you don't meet all the qualifications for. When I was job searching with only two years of experience under my belt, I still applied for roles that required candidates to have three to five years of experience, especially if the job description listed skills that I had already developed. In these cases, I used the overall reading and balance of the job description to assess whether I'd be likely to succeed in the position despite not meeting the experience requirements. If I thought that I would succeed in and was genuinely interested in the role, then I would go ahead and apply anyway. However, if a job description called for ten years of experience while I only had two, I would not apply, regardless of how interesting it sounded or whether I thought I could succeed.

As with many things in life, determining whether you qualify for a job or whether or not to apply for a job is a balancing act. You should consider the job description holistically and assess whether you are ready, willing, and able to carry out the responsibilities of the role. The answer might not always be clear. But like the New York Lottery says, "Hey, you never know!" So, if you are feeling confident, shoot your shot and go for it, because *Hey, you never know!*

Step 5: Prepare for Interviews

There will come a point in your job search where you have already applied to everything that you're interested in, and there are no new job postings that pique your interest. This is when the waiting game truly begins.

Check inbox. 0 new emails. Refreshes inbox. 0 new emails. Refreshes inbox again. Still 0 new emails. Repeat. Repeat. Repeat.

One proactive step you can take to distract yourself from what feels like endless waiting is to begin to prepare for interviews. There different ways to do interview prep once you have some legal and professional experience. Perhaps the easiest way to start is by coming up with examples that connect your most recent professional experience to the role you are applying for. The more experience you have, the more connections you can make. These real-life examples are also a good way to convey important soft skills you possess that are relevant to the role. For example, to show that I am an effective communicator, I might describe the time I helped to implement a process that had been updated to comply with sanctions regulations, and how, as the sanctions expert, I was responsible for answering any questions my colleagues had about the new process. Interviews are largely about telling your story and having a conversation with the person who is interviewing you.

Also be sure to review frequently asked interview questions (FAQs). You can search for these online. Common examples of FAQs are: What your greatest strengths? What your greatest weaknesses? Tell me about a time you worked on a challenging project. Describe a time when you had to work with a difficult team or individual and how you handled it. And so on and so forth. One of the top FAQ interview questions is simply "Tell me about yourself." *5'10, brown hair, blue eyes, killer smile, loves pina coladas and getting caught in the rain, shy at first but super fun once you get to know me. Oh wait, not that information?* In all seriousness, though, this question is a wonderful opportunity for you as a young lawyer to explain how your experiences and career goals make you the right fit for this new role. In preparing my own "tell me about yourself" response, I focused on three things: (1) my education, (2) my work experience, and (3) my personality and work ethic. I then took things a step further and tied my response to the basic job qualifications (i.e., I explained why I could competently do the job) and used it in my overall sales pitch (i.e., I used it to explain why they should pick me).

My "tell me about yourself" practice response went something like this:

> *Interviewer: So, John, let's kick this interview off. Tell me about yourself to get us started.*
>
> *Me: Sure thing. So, my name is John Reilly, and I'm a lawyer who has been working as a sanctions compliance associate focusing on U.S. and E.U. sanctions regulations. I graduated from Brooklyn Law School in 2019, and during my time in law school, I took international law classes and was a member of the International Law Society. That was the area of law that I was most interested in during law school, so I was happy to find a job after law school at Société Genérale as a sanctions compliance associate, where I was able to continue to focus on U.S. and international sanctions regulations and how they impact the bank. As I have continued to grow in the sanctions space, I have been eager to take on additional roles and responsibilities in the sanctions field in a legal setting, so when I saw this job posting, I was eager to put my application together and submit it. As a lawyer who works in the sanctions field, I know that I will not only be able to perform the job but I will also be able to collaborate well with others to help the team succeed. In my previous experiences, my positive attitude, my dedicated work ethic, and my desire to continue learning every day made me a*

valuable member of the teams that I worked with. I am looking forward to discussing that more with you today and showing how my education, experiences, and personality are a good fit for your company.

When it comes to prioritizing questions for interview prep, the "tell me about yourself" question should be at the top of the list. Once you've worked out your response to this question, then you can start to prepare answers to other common interview questions and choose which stories you want to tell. You might even find that your answer to this question can act as a North Star, guiding your responses to other questions about yourself.

You'll also need to prepare questions that you can ask the interviewer about the role and the company. This is a critical stage in every interview. After the interviewer has finished asking their questions, they will normally ask if you have any of your own. In this moment, you can either fall flat or differentiate yourself and convey your interest. An interviewer is likely to interpret a lack of questions as a lack of interest, so be sure to always have some prepared in advance.

For me, a good rule of thumb is to have at least five questions prepared for your interviewer. These can be a mix of general questions that are appropriate in almost any interview and specific and nuanced questions pertaining to that particular role or company. For example, you could ask your interviewer about their favorite and least favorite parts of their job, or their favorite and least favorite aspects of working at the company. You could ask them how they would define success for someone in this role, or how a new employee could demonstrate success within the first few months of being hired. If you need ideas for more specific questions, the company website is a great place to start. There, you might find a wealth of information, including news updates about company employees, current projects, or recent successes or failures. After you've checked out their website, it's a good idea to search the internet for recent news articles about the company that might give you insight into how it is perceived from the outside. And last but not least, if you haven't done so already (and you should have—see Step 3 above), turn to your network—see if any of your network connections work at the company, and reach out to them. They may offer you info that leads to a great question for the interviewer.

Asking specific questions shows that you did your homework for the interview. For example, if I were interviewing for a sanctions position, I might say something like "I saw on the company website that you've recently expanded into the artificial intelligence area. What role did the sanctions team play in helping get that project across the finish line?" or "I saw that John Smith was appointed as the new Chief Compliance Officer. How closely do you work with him, and what has that experience been like for you?"

Why do I suggest having at least five questions prepared? Because it's possible that some of the questions you've prepared in advance for the interviewer will be answered during the interview itself. So, using an example from above, if the interviewer already said that she works with the new CCO and really likes him, I'm not going to end the interview by asking that question. If that's the only question I prepared, I might be in trouble. But if I have several backup questions, I can just ask one of those instead.

I've also found myself in interviews where half an hour or an hour has been blocked off for the meeting, yet the interviewer only speaks for a few brief minutes. They explain their role and the role that I'm interviewing for and then leave the rest of the interview open-ended, expecting me to ask questions. This type of situation can be intimidating, but having a variety of prepared questions to help carry the conversation along can really help to mitigate some of the stress. The stories they tell in response to your prepared questions may lead to anecdotes or additional questions that flow naturally from the conversation.

When you are prepared for an interview, you are more likely to be confident. When you are confident, you are more likely to answer questions clearly, completely, and authentically. Preparation makes it possible to put your best foot forward during an interview. You won't be able to anticipate every question and, sometimes, you may even be asked curveball questions. But thorough preparation can help you to develop a pool of experiences that you can draw from in crafting well-reasoned responses on the spot.

Accepting (and Negotiating) Job Offers

So I filtered through the jobs that I want to apply for... check.

I created killer resumes that were tailored to those jobs... check.

I prepared for and crushed all the interviews I've had... check.

Now there's only one thing left to do—accept the best job offer! Woohoo!

Sometimes the application process for a job can be really drawn out. More often than not, every stage of the interview process is separated by a few weeks. This means it might be months before you land a job offer.

Find a job you are interested in and apply to it... wait a few weeks.

Hear back from the recruiter that the team may want to interview you... wait a few weeks.

Finally schedule an interview with the hiring manager... wait a few weeks.

Conduct any second or third round interviews with senior management... wait a few weeks.

Finally get a job offer—and the kicker is that the company would love a response as soon as you possibly could provide one.

After receiving an offer, there are steps you can take to help you evaluate it and make the best decision for your career.

Sometimes, an offer initially may be communicated orally; however, an offer should be more formally and seriously considered once it is made in writing. Some (obvious) considerations are title of the role, team/management structure, salary and bonus, benefits, and work environment (remote/hybrid/in-person). Even before you receive any formal job offers, though, it may be helpful to create a table or Excel spreadsheet to track and compare each potential job to your current job, or in the case of multiple offers, to one another. List the individual considerations vertically down the left side of the chart, then add labels for your current job and any potential jobs horizontally across the top of the chart, like this:

	Current Job	Potential Job 1	Potential Job 2	Potential Job 3	Potential Job 4	Potential Job 5
Salary						
Bonus						
Total Comp						
Work Location						
PTO						
401 K						
Other Benefits						
Application Status						

This exercise is even a great way to help you identify your priorities while you wait for job offers to come in. For example, maybe it helps you realize that being fully remote is more important than a modest pay increase if that increase means you have to come into the office every week. But maybe you also realize that you could live with a hybrid role if the position came with a large pay increase. Or maybe you realize that you prioritize great benefits (e.g., health insurance, lots of PTO, 401K matching) more than a salary increase.

But back to job offers. You could find yourself in a dilemma where you receive more than one job offer and can't make a decision. Which do you accept? (*Okay, maybe dilemma is a strong word to use here... more like some people may be lucky to have these options.)*

When I was still employed at Société Genérale and searching for my next job, I found about ten or so job postings that really excited me. Within a few months, I had lined up around four preliminary HR calls and first-round interviews. For three of those roles, I advanced to second- and third-round interviews. One company ultimately chose another candidate, another made me an offer, and the third was taking a while to respond. The offer I received came from a small financial technology company that was growing their regulatory practice. They were looking for someone with sanctions and regulatory experience who was open to learning more about corporate and in-house counsel responsibilities. The job I was still waiting on was a regulatory council position at a credit card company (Mastercard). In that role, I would be working as sanctions counsel and expanding my knowledge in export controls and anti-money laundering. From a subject matter perspective, both interested me. In terms of benefits, the financial technology company had some major pros: it offered a higher salary than my current job and unlimited PTO, and it was fully remote. But Mastercard had major pros as well: it offered a significantly higher salary than my current job, an extremely generous 401K match, generous PTO and sick days, and a four-days-work-from home/one-day-in-the-office hybrid schedule.

When I received the financial technology company's offer, I was excited and nervous at the same time. I was excited because I knew that it would be a good next step in my career. But I was nervous because I didn't want to make a decision before hearing back from Mastercard. I decided to tell them that I had been interviewing with other companies and wanted to wait for those decisions before accepting or declining their offer. They understood, and we agreed to touch base in a few days. I then reached out to Mastercard's HR representative, explained the situation, and asked whether they could give me their decision within the next few days. As someone unfamiliar with job negotiations, revealing this information did not feel normal to me. I felt like I was giving them information I shouldn't be.

Don't let any of these companies know that you're interviewing for other jobs. It is like cheating! You have to make them feel like they are special and the only one so that they hire you!

The Mastercard HR representative thanked me for keeping her in the loop and promised to get back to me shortly. Sure enough, the next day I received their written offer. Again I felt excitement and nervousness run through my body.

My brain: This is great! I have options!

Also my brain: What am I going to do?! Who am I going to tell yes?! Who am I going to tell no?! I'M NERVOUS!!!

Once I had both written offers, I crunched the numbers for salary and benefits. Mastercard's salary offer came in significantly higher, and their 401K benefits were stronger; however, the financial technology company's PTO policy was better, and the role was fully remote. After comparing the offers side by side, I ultimately decided that higher pay and a better 401K matching plan were more important to me than being fully remote. I let my partner and family know that I had received two offers and had made my decision. *It was exciting to let them know that I was actually going to accept an offer!*

But first I had to call the financial technology company and tell them that I had decided to accept another offer. This felt awkward to me. But things took an unexpected turn when they offered to match Mastercard's salary because they really wanted me to work with them. This was simultaneously flattering and anxiety-inducing.

Would I reconsider the job offer now? Does this change things for me? I need to let it sit for a little bit. I'M NOT SURE!

I said that I needed a few days to consider their new offer. Afterward, I let Mastercard know that another company had just matched their salary offer and asked whether Mastercard would consider raising their original offer. At this point, I felt like I was in the driver's seat and had some leverage. Mastercard ultimately counteroffered with a salary that was 3 percent higher than their original offer. *Three percent more? Wow! Something to think about!*

I went back and compared my two offers again. I found that I kept going back to Mastercard's better 401K benefits. Everything else was about equal—similar salaries, one day in the office versus no days in the office. I also started to consider that Mastercard, as a larger company, would offer more growth opportunity. Ultimately, I accepted the job with Mastercard. It felt great to hear from the HR representative and hiring manager, who both let me know how excited they were to have me aboard. *Mission accomplished! You are ready to start your new job!*

After this process, my confidence was soaring. I felt so different from where I was mentally just two and a half years prior. I no longer felt like an incompetent person with no skills to offer (*side note: that was not true then, but it was how I felt*). Instead, I felt like a badass lawyer who was ready to take on new challenges and continue growing. *Of course you feel like a badass lawyer who is ready to take on new challenges—because you are a badass lawyer who's ready to take on new challenges!*

Upon accepting my new position, I put in my notice at Société Genérale, thanked my teammates and other colleagues for being so great, and then started to prepare for the new challenge ahead.

10

Starting Your Second (or Third?) Legal Job: Here We Go Again!

Bring what you know and be ready to work.

New computer... check.

New headset... check.

Same old first day at a new job nerves... check.

Prior to my start date, Mastercard sent me a new laptop, headset, phone, and other documents to help get me up and running. When my start date finally arrived, I sat down at my desk in my apartment, dressed in a crisp, white, button-up shirt (*and my finest Nike basketball shorts*), and... realized that I had nothing to work on yet. It felt weird to sit there with no work items or agenda. Even on my last day at Société Genérale, I spent the whole day on my computer, wrapping up last-minute projects. But now, I had a phone and computer that weren't even set up. (*The work version of syllabus week, I'll take it!*) So I called some folks to help get my technology situation squared away and then touched base with my new manager. He sent over a few documents for me to review about Mastercard and the Regulatory Affairs team, and he advised me that it might be a while before I was completely up and running. But he also encouraged me to be proactive during this time.

During those first few weeks, I took many steps to help onboard and integrate myself with my new team. I proactively reached out to colleagues to introduce myself, reviewed the company policies and intranet, and kept abreast of new sanctions updates and regulations.

Reaching out to colleagues to introduce myself. To help me get started, my manager directed me to the organizational chart and pointed out a number of people he worked with on a daily basis. My introductory emails led to Teams calls or other calls that made it easier to get to know my new colleagues. Introducing myself to colleagues in this manner turned out to be a very helpful exercise. It helped me to become more familiar with Mastercard's corporate and team structure. I learned about different business lines and how they operate. I learned about how these teams previously interacted with sanctions counsel and what type of sanctions issues have been presented to them in the past. I was able to explain my background and ask how I could be helpful moving forward. I could better understand how to integrate myself as counsel for the various business lines within the company. As someone who was very eager to hit the ground running, this gave me something to do during the first few weeks when I wasn't overly busy.

Reviewing company policies and intranet. *Policies and procedures? Sounds riveting!* For many folks, reviewing team policies and procedures can feel like a check-the-box exercise. They may be skimmed and scanned more than actually read. But in my mind, this is a valuable exercise. Carefully reading the policies and procedures provided helpful background on how the team operated when it came to legal and risk-based sanctions issues, and I was able to identify who were the appropriate contacts to reach out to in certain situations. I took notes on all of this so that, when a particular issue popped up in the future, I could independently reach out to the appropriate individual(s) and know the correct next-steps to take, without having to trouble my manager.

Keeping abreast of new updates in my field. While I was being onboarded and adjusting to my new role, I made sure to stay up to date on any new developments in sanctions regulations, export controls, and anti-money laundering regulations. I knew from my experience at Société Genérale that once new sanctions developments were reported in the news, different business lines were likely to tap the sanctions team with questions about policies and procedures to assess whether certain actions were permissible. By keeping my knowledge current, I would be prepared when it mattered. I also spent time reading the news to learn more about export controls and anti-money laundering regulations, as these were topics that I had a basic understanding of but was not yet an expert in. To help keep track of any updates, I created a Word doc containing notes and links to relevant updates. This document could serve as a quick reference guide if needed.

Taking these steps during my first few weeks, when I didn't yet have a heavy workload, was a way to set myself up for success once my workload did increase. I used my free time wisely, preparing for questions or issues that could one day arise. Additionally, on a personal level, taking these steps helped from a "first day/week/month nerves" perspective. Rather than twiddle my thumbs during this slow time, I kept my mind busy with learning new materials and meeting new colleagues.

Getting Started on Real Work

Slowly but surely, different work streams and responsibilities started to be handed off to me. This was, again, both exciting and slightly nerve-wracking. *Starting to notice any themes?* It was my first time in a legal counsel role, and I wanted to be sure that I was providing sound advice. I was fortunate that my manager was receptive to answering all of my questions. He reasoned that the more questions I asked up front, the faster I would be brought up to speed, and the easier his life would become. Having this assurance from him helped to ease some of my anxiety.

In my new role, I was working closely with the sanctions compliance team. Based on my prior experience with sanctions compliance, I was aware of the different issues and challenges they deal with, and I had already begun to think of ways to help them from a legal perspective, which excited me. I enjoyed keeping them apprised of new regulations and providing advice as needed. My manager and I had established a process where I was free to provide advice without first running it by him as long as I was confident of the answer. But for questions that involved risk judgment or presented a novel, complex issue, I should consult with him and figure out the appropriate next steps.

I was also able to use some of the skills I had developed in my previous roles to help build my own projects and add value to the team. How? For starters, I got involved with some metrics projects. *More metrics? For real?!* During the interview process, I had talked about my metrics responsibilities at Société Genérale, so my manager knew it was an area I had experience in. Once he decided that he wanted to start compiling team metrics, he came to me. He told me the different metrics that he wanted to see, and I offered ways to start collecting the data and suggested that the data be presented to him and management on a quarterly basis. Because he had not done this type of project before, he gave me the freedom to do what I needed to do and keep him posted as needed. This was an opportunity for me to build my brand and utilize my unique skillset, and it was exciting. I was creating value and was showing that I could be a high-producing member of the team.

Nevertheless, there still was a lot for me to learn, from both a company perspective and legal perspective. From a company perspective, I had to learn to deal with having many different people come to me with questions about many different types of sanctions issues. Their questions required me to conduct research and craft nuanced responses, which was quite different from the transactional work I was doing at Société Genérale. There was definitely a learning curve, but I developed a two-step process to help me address their issues. Step one was to take the first crack at drafting a solution. I'd use my existing knowledge and whatever resources I had to craft the best answer I could. Step two was to confer with my manager and see whether he agreed with the solution came up with. Sometimes, he would provide additional insight or context based on previous experience he had, but he always appreciated that I would show up with a well thought out draft. From a personal perspective, I had to learn that not being able to provide immediate answers all the time is okay. I'd love to be able to answer every question on the spot, but that is just not how being a lawyer works. (*At least not yet for me!*) It took time for me to adjust to that reality.

I knew I was integrating well with my new team when folks from other teams or my manager would pick up the phone and call me to bounce certain sanctions questions off of me. Sometimes they just wanted a second opinion, sometimes they wanted to know if I had any additional context. It was satisfying to know that my thoughts and insight were valuable to the team. *Hey, you're a lawyer! That's your job! You're doing it! You're providing legal advice!*

Giving Yourself Time to Adjust to Your New Job

Am I doing this new job well? Am I qualified for this? Did I make the jump at the right time? Is this working out? Do I miss my old job?

When I was still new, it was normal for me to go through rapid fire questions like these, from time to time. Starting a new job is a big life change requiring you to make many adjustments. It can be easy to succumb to the doubt that creeps in when you don't know the answer to something or when you do something wrong and need to be corrected by a team member. But these are teaching moments, and they are a natural part of adjusting to a new job.

As a new lawyer, there are steps you can actively take to monitor and check in on your progress. One tool that I've used to help me gauge my progress is a 30-60-90 table. The table has three rows—labeled 30 days, 60 days, and 90 days, respectively—and two columns—one labeled "manager's comments" and another labeled "my comments." *An internal meeting if you will.* I used this table to track how well I was doing from my manager's perspective and from my own perspective. Around the 30, 60, and 90 day marks, I made sure to meet with my manager to discuss how he thought my progress was going, to touch base on the projects I was working on, and to see if there were any additional steps I should take or benchmarks I should hit as I was being onboarded. I would take notes during these meetings and then add them to my table under the "manager's comments" column. I'd also add my thoughts in the other column, including thoughts about specific projects, how much I was enjoying the work, how much I was learning, how I felt about my interactions with the team, and how I felt about my work-life balance.

Filling out this table forces you to consider both objective and subjective aspects of your job, and it shows you how or whether your perception and reaction to your job is changing over time. On my 30-60-90 table, for example, I could see that my overall experience was positive and that my doubt and anxiety were much higher on day 30 than on days 60 or 90. I could also see that there were no "Oh no, I've made a mistake!" moments like I had at the real estate law firm. *My real estate law firm experience helped to put every other job in perspective!* Seeing my positive growth and development over time was reassuring to me.

	Manager's comments	**My comments**
30 days		
60 days		
90 days		

If creating a 30-60-90 table isn't your thing, a more informal alternative could be to take notes and save them in a Word doc or Notes app. Spending a few minutes at the end of the every work-week to record what you're working on and the skills you're developing is a good way to track your progress. This exercise can also help you to assess how well you're adjusting to your role and your overall feelings about the position. I wish that I had done this type of reflective exercise when I was working at the real estate law firm.

It should be said that no job is perfect, and there definitely will be hard days and hard weeks no matter where you work. But, by keeping weekly notes, you might be able to recognize which teams, projects, or colleagues make your week easier or harder. Identifying these trends can allow you to actively prepare for certain colleagues or situations.

Adjusting to a new job is not a check-the-box exercise or something that can be done in one week. (*No matter how much I wish it was that easy!*) It takes lots of action to integrate into a new role. Whether you decide to create a 30-60-90 table or keep informal notes, the point is to be able to periodically look back at your progress and evaluate how things are going and how you feel. Knowing which aspects of your job you enjoy, which you don't necessarily enjoy, and which you need to work on can help you to make better decisions as you move forward in your career. Becoming integrated in your new role is the first step to succeeding. *You can do it!*

11

Looking Ahead: Life Audit

Okay, now that I've passed the bar, *got a job in real estate, hated it, got a new job in the sanctions field, applied for a new job, got a new job, and adjusted to it... what do I do next? Excel at my new job? Get a promotion? Become the CEO? Achieve world domination? Retire?*

The answer to these questions is yes (obviously). However, (sadly) I haven't achieved everything yet. But be on the lookout for my next book!

I got the idea for this book a few weeks after leaving the real estate firm (*and crying next to Elmo in Times Square*). I had never felt so miserable and anxiety-ridden. I felt as though I reeked of failure. The sinking feeling in my chest felt like my new normal. As I was dealing with these emotions, applying for new jobs, and trying to get my career back on track, the question I kept coming back to was *how did I get here?*

I did everything right. College. *Check.* Law school. *Check.* Great internships. *Check.* I did all the things I was supposed to do to find a fulfilling career. And yet, there I was, crying next to Elmo in Times Square. But it was during this time, when I was at my lowest, that I started to realize that success involves more than checking boxes. When I took a step back, I could see all the other positive aspects of my life. I had a loving partner, amazing family, and the best friends. I had my health and could work out. My financial situation as an unemployed person wasn't amazing, but it also wasn't dire. I still had a roof over my head, I had recently traveled, and I had more time for my hobbies. When I looked at my life from this perspective, all of a sudden my career issues did not feel insurmountable. *Sure, I need to find a new job, but with so many good things going for me in other parts of my life, maybe I will get through this.*

Though I didn't realize it at the time, what I was doing when I looked at the big picture was conducting a life audit. A life audit is a process in which you identify different aspects of your life, break them down into smaller components, and then rate how satisfied you are with each, enabling you to see what you're content with what you need to improve on and work at.

To start a life audit, you must first identify which aspects of your life to address. The ones I chose were (*in no particular order)* (1) career, (2) finances, (3) physical health, (4) mental health, (5) romantic relationship, (6) relationships with friends and family, (7) hobbies/spare time, and (8) living situation. *Feel like there should be more components? Google search "life audit" to read up on all the other components that could possibly be included here.*

Below is an example of a life audit chart. Filling it out can help you to organize your thoughts and begin the life audit process. Each slice of the pie represents an aspect of your life that you are evaluating, and there are 10 lines within each slice, basically representing a 1–10 scale. The more lines you shade in within a given slice, the happier you are. The fewer lines, the more dissatisfied you are.

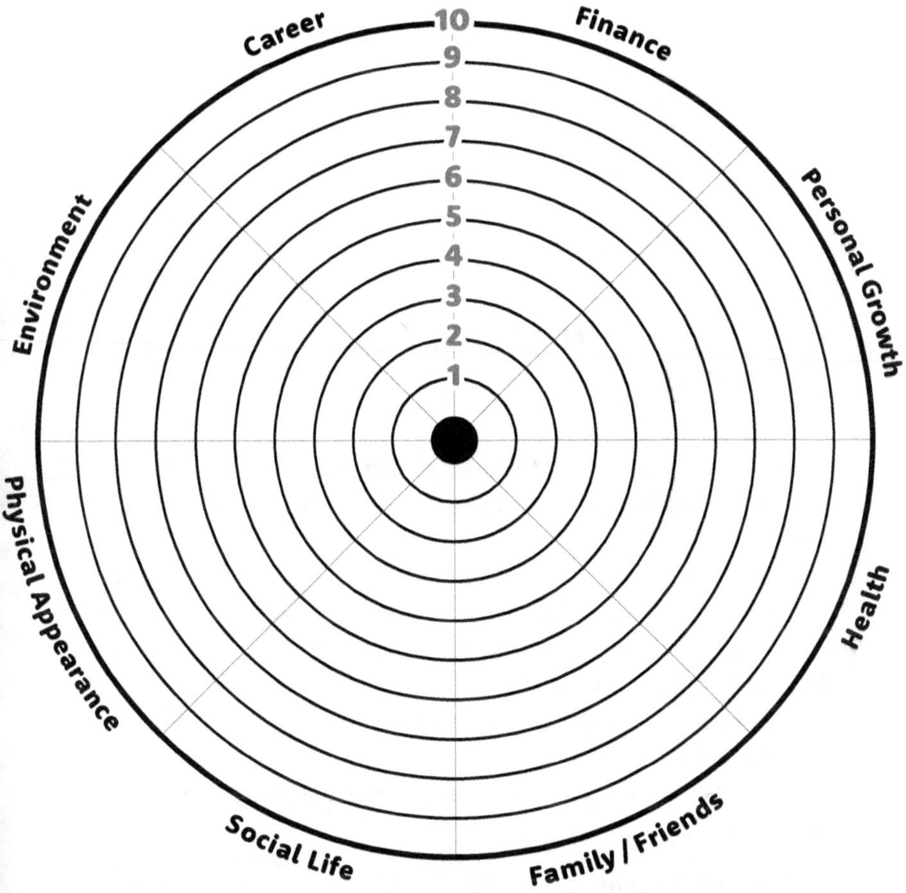

Based on *How to Do a Life Audit with the Wheel of Life*, Sunday Rainday (June 26, 2022), https://www.sundayrainday.com/how-to-do-a-life-audit-with-the-wheel-of-life/.

The first time you fill out your life audit chart will be something of a gut check. *What is your initial sense of how things are going?* As you reflect more on each component, you can make changes and hone your assessments. There are different ways to approach this process. For example, you could create your life audit chart and then update it as needed. Alternatively, you could create your initial life audit chart, save it, create interim charts or a final chart (*final for now, not forever*) that serve as snapshots of your perceptions at different points in the process, and then compare your charts with one another to see how your perceptions have changed over time.

Below, I break down my review of the career aspect of my life audit. Later, I include questions relevant to other components of the life audit that you might find helpful.

Life Audit: Career

You spend more time during the week with the people you work with than your family!

My workday is never 9 to 5—it's always longer!

Are you checking your work email on the weekend again? Put that phone away!

For most lawyers, work is all-encompassing. It impacts emotional, physical, and financial well-being. From this perspective, ensuring that your career aligns with your values and brings you happiness is a paramount task.

To begin your career audit, do a gut check. Ask yourself "How am I feeling about my career and job right now?" Write down whatever comes to mind, and then rate this aspect of your life on a scale of one to ten.

> *I feel like things are going well. I have learned a lot about sanctions law, I'm interested in learning more about sanctions law, I like my team, and I can see myself growing in this position. I rate this area of my life as a nine.*

OR

> *Things are going really horribly. I'm not happy. I do not like the people I work with. I dread work every day. I don't like real estate that much. I rate this area of my life as a one.*

Writing down how you feel when you do this gut check is an important first step in your career audit. It forces you to make a broad assessment ("things are going well" or "things could be better") that you can then dissect and break down into smaller component parts—kind of like a pros and cons list. Once you dig deeper into why you are feeling a certain way, you may realize that the reasons for your feelings are overwhelmingly obvious. But, other times, you may end up seeing that things are better (*or worse*) than your initial gut check led you to believe.

Learning about sanctions law energizes me. I am excited by learning more about the field, and I enjoy the parts of my day when I get to teach other members of the company about sound sanctions practices.

I am happy that I am building off my law school experience and developing my career as a lawyer. I know that I am building valuable skills that will help me in my career down the line.

Sometimes I wish I could work fewer hours, but I might experience the same issue at whatever job I have. I still agree with my original rating of nine.

OR

This job in real estate does not align with my values. The folks here are not kind to each other. The culture doesn't reflect a growth mindset or promote having compassion for other colleagues. I do not feel passionately about real estate. I think transactional real estate skills would be good to have as a lawyer, but not in this environment. Can I rate this area of my life below one? Zero? Negative ten? Negative infinity?!

Sometimes, the answers will flow out naturally as new ideas come to mind. But if they don't, asking yourself more pointed questions can help to get the juices flowing and your ideas down on paper. Some examples are:

- Is my job aligned with my values? (What are my career values?)
- Do I enjoy working with my work colleagues? (Why or why not?)

- Do I feel valued by my company? (Why or why not?)
- Do I like my work now? (Why or why not?)
- Do I like the direction of my career trajectory? (Why or why not?)
- Am I at a dead end of career growth in this position? (Why or why not?)
- Do I feel like it is time to move on? (Why or why not?)

Asking these questions and rating your feelings can help you to more intentionally and set goals for and plan for the future.

I am currently happy with my job and want to grow in this position and with this company. My goal is to continue taking on more work, to work closely with my manager on new projects so that I can learn from him, and to be promoted within two years.

OR

I need to leave this job ASAP and find something else that is more aligned with my values and career goals. Note to self: start looking into other career options!!!

The more specific and measurable your goals, the easier it will be to make a plan and achieve them. After identifying areas that are going well and areas that need improvement, you can decide how best to tackle them. Maybe you just need to make small tweaks in your day-to-day routine or discuss new work opportunities with your manager. But maybe this exercise turns out to be a wakeup call requiring a complete 180 or different career path.

As I've emphasized (or tried to) throughout this book, how well (or not) things are going in your career can majorly impact other areas of your life—this is particularly true for lawyers, who put in so much time and effort (*and blood, sweat, and tears—lots of tears*) into law school and passing the bar. Finding a legal career that is fulfilling, aligns with your values, and makes you want to get up in the morning is one of the most important things you can do for your overall well-being. That's why taking the time to perform a career audit is a gift you give yourself. It can lead you toward different possibilities and outcomes that you otherwise may not have thought about. This exercise not only allows you to pinpoint where you are on your career trajectory but encourages you to consider others possible paths and opportunities so that you can chart the best course forward. One of the great things about a career audit is that you can repeat the process over and over again as you grow in your career and change over time.

Life Audit: All Other Areas

Originally, I had planned to complete my current life audit and share it here with you. But, upon further consideration, I decided it was better not to. *Aw, man! Are you sure you don't want to share all the riveting details about your finances and romantic relationship?!* Instead, I'd like to share some potential questions relating to other life areas that might be useful for those of you who want to perform a full life audit.

Finances

- How do I feel about my finances right now? What would I rate them on a 1–10 scale?
- How much money do I make monthly? Can I live off of this amount?
- Do I have a budget? Am I sticking to it?
- Do I have debt? Do I have a plan to pay it off?
- Are there things I should spend less money on? More money on?
- Am I spending beyond my means?
- Are there ways to increase my income on a monthly basis?
- Am I able to save money on a monthly basis?
- Am I happy with my current financial state?

Physical Health

- How do I feel about my physical health right now? What would I rate it on a 1–10 scale?
- Do I exercise regularly? Sporadically? Never?
- Are there physical activities I enjoy? Do I do these activities regularly?
- Are there ways to incorporate more physical activity into my daily life?
- Am I managing any chronic illnesses?
- Am I eating a healthy diet?
- Am I finding a balance between cooking for myself and eating out/ordering takeout?
- Am I getting annual check ups/screenings?
- Am I getting enough sleep?

Mental Health

- How do I feel about my mental health? What would I rate it on a 1–10 scale?
- Am I taking care of my mental health and seeking help if needed?
- Are stress and anxiety overwhelming me? Are they manageable?
- Am I managing stress and anxiety in a healthy way?
- Am I taking steps to maintain a healthy work-life balance?
- Am I practicing self-care and setting aside time for relaxation?
- Am I taking time for self-reflection and meditation on a daily basis? On a monthly basis? Ever?

Romantic Relationship

- How do I feel about my romantic relationship? What would I rate it on a 1–10 scale?

- Am I in a healthy and fulfilling romantic relationship? Am I actively seeking one out? Do I want to?
- Do my partner and I communicate effectively?
- Do my partner and I resolve conflicts in a constructive manner? Can we resolve issues without intentionally hurting (verbally, physically, or otherwise) each other?
- Do my goals and my partner's goals (family, work, social life, financial) align?
- How do I want to continue growing with my partner?
- Do my partner and I make time to connect on a deeper level?

Relationships with Friends and Family

- How do I feel about my relationships with friends and family? What would I rate them on a 1–10 scale?
- Am I maintaining healthy and fulfilling relationships with friends and family?
- Am I making time for the people who are important to me? Are they making time for me?
- Am I calling/visiting/spending time with friends and family periodically, on a weekly, monthly, or quarterly basis?
- Am I effectively communicating with my friends and family? Am I setting boundaries when appropriate?
- Am I actively seeking out new relationships with friends and family? Am I making time to do this?

Hobbies/Spare Time

- How do I feel about my hobbies and how I spend my spare time? What would I rate them on a 1–10 scale?
- Am I making time for hobbies and activities that bring me joy?
- Can I build more time into my schedule for hobbies or spare time?

- Am I periodically trying new activities that I might enjoy? Am I trying new activities that may take me outside of my comfort zone?
- Am I taking time to try new activities by myself? Am I taking time to try new activities with friends and family?
- Am I challenging myself to learn new skills? Am I challenging myself to pick up old skills that I have not practiced in a long time?
- Am I making time to relax and recharge? Am I wasting time?
- Am I setting time aside to take care of myself?
- Am I traveling to different places?
- Am I planning for activities that require me to go outside of my house/neighborhood? Am I planning activities that I can do at home?

Living Situation

- How do I feel about my living situation? What would I rate it on a 1–10 scale?
- Am I happy with my current living situation?
- Is my space my sanctuary?
- Do I love my space? Neighborhood? City? State?
- Am I living in a healthy and safe environment?
- Do I live near friends and family?
- Am I able to easily access resources and amenities that I need?
- Do I enjoy being in my space? Do I enjoy having friends and family over?

12
Conclusion

This is the first book that I've ever written, so I'm not sure how it is supposed to end. And to be completely candid, I was not sure how it was supposed to start or progress either. I just knew from the get-go that I had a story to tell that I wanted to put in writing. So I used every evening, weekend, and moment of free time that I had to put it all together, one word and one page at a time. And now it is done!

When I graduated from Brooklyn Law School on May 17th, 2019, I was full of hope and excitement. I had just completed seven years of post-secondary education (and a lifetime of education before that), and I was ready to take on the world. But I had no idea that I would be walking out of my graduation ceremony and into a bunch of professional obstacles that would knock me down, challenge me, make me question my decision to pursue a career as a lawyer, and ultimately, teach me that I can get knocked down and get right back up again.

Being a lawyer is hard work. It is not a destination but rather a journey. *Corny, I know, but please bear with me.* And part of that journey is making choices every day that that impact how and in what ways you want your career to grow. I could have stayed at my first post-law school job for at least two more years and been miserable every day. But I did not. After some self-reflection, conversations with loved ones, and, as you know, tears, I decided to make the jump to a new job and industry that I was more interested in. It was a new path that, although scary and uncertain at times, offered a step up and a way to move forward from the misery that had been consuming me.

At the beginning of this career journey, I felt stuck. I felt alone. I felt isolated. And while I may have been stuck, alone, and isolated within the four walls of the law firm I was at, these feelings did not have to define or apply to my career trajectory or my life in general. I had great law school classmates, professors, mentors, family, friends, and the most wonderful partner. I had the best people in my corner to support me during this difficult time, and that helped me overcome the shame, fear, and indecisiveness I was feeling. I had the support system and the power to choose to pursue a career more aligned with my interests and goals.

What I learned from this experience is that you need to listen to your gut. At that time in my life, I was dealing with conflicting emotions. On the one hand, I had secured a flashy job in Manhattan as a commercial real estate lawyer, just like I dreamed. *How could I give it up?* On the other hand, once I saw how miserable everybody was and realized how miserable that made me, I could barely stomach the thought of waking up and heading to the office every day. *How could I stay?* Ultimately (and somewhat begrudgingly), I took a leap of faith by quitting my secure job to find something new. Through that action, and countless others since, I have come to understand that the trajectory of my career and my life is determined by decisions that I make. Every decision forms and informs the paths we take. Sometimes we pick the wrong one. And that is okay. We can still move forward to the next fork in the road and choose to go down a completely new one. No path is guaranteed to be correct, and so we have to keep going until we find the path that makes us feel happiest, most confident, and most secure.

I have been out of law school for just a few years now. In that time, I had a job I hated, found a job I liked, and then found a different job that I liked even more—and I haven't even made it to my five-year law school reunion yet. In this short amount of time, I encountered all sorts of trials and tribulations that could have tripped me up as a new lawyer trying to find my way. But I am fortunate and grateful that each hurdle and difficult predicament that

I overcame has led me to the path that I am on now. Today, I am a more confident lawyer because of choices I made. I understand that my career trajectory is my decision, and that so long as I play an active role in developing my skills and talents, I can grow into any role that I take on. If you find yourself crying in Times Square next to Elmo because your job is making you miserable and you do not know what you are doing with your career, my advice to you is this: *keep going*. This is just the beginning of the road, not the end. You can do it.

Acknowledgments

This book is a product of so much love and mentorship from all the most wonderful people.

First and foremost, I would like to thank my husband, Jonathan, and my parents, Donna and John, for being my rocks. You cared for me and picked me up during the hardest times and cheered me on during the best times, and for that I will always be grateful. You are my everything.

To the best mentor ever, Professor Marsha Garrison: Thank you for letting me sit in your office hours, for extremely long periods of time, all throughout law school but especially during my 3L year. You encouraged me to write law review articles and books and reminded me that I have a point of view worth sharing. Thank you for also helping to read, review, and edit this project. I will always be indebted to you for helping me find my professional voice. You are the best.

To the best professors, Flora Midwood, Shane Dizon, and Heidi Brown: Thank you for bringing me on to teach bar prep and legal analysis courses at Brooklyn Law School, encouraging me to write, and guiding me through the writing process. These opportunities have allowed me to reach for new heights that I did not think were possible and to own my authentic and professional path. Thank you for everything!

To my whole family, especially my sisters, Jennifer and Jessica, my cousins, Catherine and Jean, and my besties, Deirdre and Sophia—thank you for always being there for me and being the best! Love you all!

Last but certainly not least, thank you to the team at Carolina Academic Press for making the publication of this book a reality—Carol McGeehan, Ryland Bowman, Jennifer Nuzzi, Erin Matthews, Jessica Curtis, Kerri Hughes, Tasha Gervais, Steve Oliva, and all the other folks who worked on this publication: thank you for the time, guidance, and passion you put into getting this book published. Looking forward to working with you on the next one!

Index

About the Author

COURTESY OF THE AUTHOR

John W. Reilly is a lawyer, professor, and writer dedicated to guiding new legal professionals. A graduate of the College of the Holy Cross and Brooklyn Law School, John began his career as a Real Estate Law Associate, only to encounter unexpected challenges that reshaped his understanding of the profession. In *The Brand-New Lawyer's Guide to Passing the Bar, Learning the Trade, and Building a Sustainable Career*, he candidly shares his journey. From dilemmas to ultimate success, he offers vital insights for new lawyers navigating a legal career and personal well-being. When not practicing law, teaching, or writing, John enjoys running, exploring new restaurants, listening to *reputation* by Taylor Swift, and watching *Below Deck* on the couch with his husband, Jonathan. You can reach out to John at JWRisWriting@gmail.com.